Children's Drawing and Writing

D1612292

20 17001 934

NEW COLLEGE, SWINDON

Routledge Research in Education

For a full list of titles in this series, please visit www.routledge.com

11. Policy Discourses, Gender, and Education
Constructing Women's Status
Elizabeth J. Allan

12. Improving Teacher Education through Action Research
Edited by Ming-Fai Hui
and David L. Grossman

13. The Politics of Structural Education Reform
Keith A. Nitta

14. Political Approaches to Educational Administration and Leadership
Edited by Eugenie A. Samier
with Adam G. Stanley

15. Structure and Agency in the Neoliberal University
Edited by Joyce E. Canaan and
Wesley Shumar

16. Postmodern Picturebooks
Play, Parody, and Self-Referentiality
Edited by Lawrence R. Sipe and
Sylvia Pantaleo

17. Play, Creativity and Digital Cultures
Edited By Rebekah Willet,
Muriel Robinson, and Jackie Marsh

18. Education and Neoliberal Globalization
Carlos Alberto Torres

19. Tracking Adult Literacy and Numeracy Skills
Findings from Longitudinal Research
Edited by Stephen Reder and
John Bynner

20. Emergent Computer Literacy
A Developmental Perspective
Helen Mele Robinson

21. Participatory Learning in the Early Years
Research and Pedagogy
Edited by Donna Berthelsen, Jo
Brownlee, and Eva Johansson

22. International Perspectives on the Goals of Universal Basic and Secondary Education
Edited by Joel E. Cohen and
Martin B. Malin

23. The Journey for Inclusive Education in the Indian Sub-Continent
Mithu Alur and Michael Bach

24. Traveller, Nomadic and Migrant Education
Edited by Patrick Alan Danaher, Máirín
Kenny, and Judith Remy Leder

25. Perspectives on Supported Collaborative Teacher Inquiry
Edited by David Slavit, Tamara
Holmlund Nelson, and Anne Kennedy

26. Mathematical Relationships in Education
Identities and Participation
Edited by Laura Black, Heather Mendick, and Yvette Solomon

27. Science, Society and Sustainability
Education and Empowerment for an Uncertain World
Edited by Donald Gray, Laura Colucci-Gray, and Elena Camino

28. The Social Psychology of the Classroom
Elisha Babad

29. Cross-Cultural Perspectives on Policy and Practice
Decolonizing Community Contexts
Edited by Jennifer Lavia and Michele Moore

30. Education and Climate Change
Living and Learning in Interesting Times
Edited by Fumiyo Kagawa and David Selby

31. Education and Poverty in Affluent Countries
Edited by Carlo Raffo, Alan Dyson, Helen Gunter, Dave Hall, Lisa Jones, and Afroditi Kalambouka

32. What's So Important About Music Education?
J. Scott Goble

33. Educational Transitions
Moving Stories from Around the World
Edited by Divya Jindal-Snape

34. Globalization, the Nation-State and the Citizen
Dilemmas and Directions for Civics and Citizenship Education
Edited by Alan Reid, Judith Gill, and Alan Sears

35. Collaboration in Education
Edited by Judith J. Slater and Ruth Ravid

36. Trust and Betrayal in Educational Administration and Leadership
Edited by Eugenie A. Samier and Michèle Schmidt

37. Teaching and Learning with Technology
Beyond Constructivism
Edited by Concetta M. Stewart, Catherine C. Schifter, and Melissa E. Markaridian Selverian

38. Gender Inclusive Engineering Education
Julie Mills, Mary Ayre, and Judith Gill

39. Intercultural and Multicultural Education
Enhancing Global Interconnectedness
Edited by Carl A. Grant and Agostino Portera

40. Systemization in Foreign Language Teaching
Monitoring Content Progression
Wilfried Decoo

41. Inclusive Education in the Middle East
Eman Gaad

42. Critical Issues in Peace and Education
Edited by Peter Pericles Trifonas and Bryan Wright

43. Children's Drawing and Writing
The Remarkable in the Unremarkable
Diane Mavers

Children's Drawing and Writing

The Remarkable in the Unremarkable

Diane Mavers

LRC
NEW COLLEGE
SWINDON
WITHDRAWN

Routledge
Taylor & Francis Group
New York   London

First published 2011
by Routledge
711 Third Avenue, New York, NY 10017

Simultaneously published in the UK
by Routledge
2 Park Square, Milton Park, Abingdon, Oxon OX14 4RN

Routledge is an imprint of the Taylor & Francis Group, an informa business

First issued in paperback 2013

© 2011 Diane Mavers   2011001934

The right of Diane Mavers to be identified as author of this work has been asserted by her in accordance with sections 77 and 78 of the Copyright, Designs and Patents Act 1988.

Typeset in Sabon by IBT Global.

All rights reserved. No part of this book may be reprinted or reproduced or utilised in any form or by any electronic, mechanical, or other means, now known or hereafter invented, including photocopying and recording, or in any information storage or retrieval system, without permission in writing from the publishers.

Trademark Notice: Product or corporate names may be trademarks or registered trademarks, and are used only for identification and explanation without intent to infringe.

Library of Congress Cataloging-in-Publication Data
Mavers, Diane.
  Children's drawing and writing : the remarkable in the unremarkable / by Diane Mavers.
    p. cm. — (Routledge research in education ; 43)
  Includes bibliographical references and index.
  1. Children's drawings. 2. Children's writings. 3. Child development. I. Title.
  LB1139.D7M27 2011
  305.231—dc22
                                          2010011174

ISBN13: 978-0-415-84644-8 (pbk)
ISBN13: 978-0-415-96155-4 (hbk)
ISBN13: 978-0-203-84436-6 (ebk)

For Martin

For Martin

Contents

List of Figures   xi
List of Tables   xv
Acknowledgments   xvii

1   A Lens on the Unremarkable   1

2   'Copying'   12

3   Ordinariness   32

4   'Getting it Wrong'   48

5   'Jumble', Shorthand and Repetition   74

6   Fleeting Texts   90

7   Remaking   105

8   From the Unremarkable to the Remarkable   124

References   131
Index   139

Figures

1.1	'Mum is my Hirow' (Shakira).	2
2.1	'Copy' of long multiplication (Tim).	17
2.2	'Copying' from the class screen.	
	a The teacher's original.	18
	b Sonita's 'copy'.	19
	c Emil's 'copy'.	19
	d Looking up (Emil).	20
2.3	'Copying' from a storybook (Nicky).	24
2.4	'Copying' from a picture dictionary.	
	a Original.	26
	b Zakariah.	26
	c Nabil.	27
	d Miguel.	27
3.1	The seasons.	
	a Rachel.	35
	b Daniel.	35
3.2	Fireworks.	
	a Katie.	37
	b Rachel.	37

3.3   Osmosis.

    a   Nathan.   43

    b   Semmy.   43

3.4   Heart message (Kerry).   46

4.1   Email exchange between Kathleen and Martin.

    a   Kathleen's initiation.   59

    b   Martin's first reply.   59

    c   Kathleen's response.   59

    d   Martin's second reply.   59

4.2   Spacing.

    a   Kathleen's spacing.   62

    b   Imposed single spacing.   62

4.3   Showing magnetic force with arrows.

    a   Tom.   68

    b   Rohana.   68

    c   Dean.   68

    d   Lily.   69

    e   Yadin.   69

5.1   'Computers in my world' (George).   76

5.2   'Computers in my world' (Amy).   78

5.3   'Computers in my world' (Oliver).   79

5.4   'Computers in my world' (Kelly).   81

5.5   'Computers in my world' (Chelsea).   85

5.6   'Computers in my world' (Amelia).   87

6.1   Dry-wipe whiteboard hypotheses.

    a   Ferah.   93 b   Lauren.   93

c   Pepe.   93

d   Hollie.   93

7.1   'Computers in my world'.

a   Jade.   108

b   Sophie.   108

7.2   Pentecost.

a   Megan.   109

b   Gareth.   109

7.3   Transcription (Ella).

a   Interactional exchange.   113

b   Ongoing contribution.   113

7.4   The storyboard (Ebony, Ambareen and Jeselle).   118

Tables

3.1   Interactions around Drawing   41

4.1   Collaborative Design (Ebony, Ambareen and Jeselle)   51

4.2   Representing Arrows Actionally (Teacher)   65

6.1   Framing the Task   95

6.2   Reporting to the Class (Hollie)   100

6.3   Modal Distribution of Meaning (Hollie)   101

7.1   Checking the Screen (Ebony and Ambareen)   121

Tables

Acknowledgments

THE MATERIALS

The materials in this book come from a range of sources:

The research project 'Shapes of representation, shapes of knowledge: from object to visualiser to page' (January–December 2007) was funded by the Centre for Excellence in Work-Based Learning for Education Professionals (WLE) at the Institute of Education, University of London (Diane Mavers project director and researcher).

The Test Bed evaluation (March 2003–December 2006) was funded by the Department for Education and Skills (DfES) and managed by the British Educational Communications and Technologies Agency (Becta). The team comprised: Bridget Somekh (Project Director), Janis Jarvis, Cathy Lewin, Diane Mavers, Sue Sing, Stephen Steadman, Derek Woodrow (Manchester Metropolitan University); Jean Underwood (Co-Director), Gayle Dillon and Sarah Forrest (Nottingham Trent University); Andy Convery (Redcar and Cleveland College); Diane Saxon (City College Manchester); and Peter Twining (Open University).

The GridClub evaluation (September 2001–January 2003) was funded by the British Educational Communications and Technologies Agency (Becta). The team comprised: Bridget Somekh (Project Director), Charmian Levin, Cathy Lewin, Diane Mavers and John Robinson (Manchester Metropolitan University); Peter Scrimshaw (Open University); and Andrew Haldane (Learning Futures).

The ImpaCT2 evaluation (October 1999–January 2002) was funded by the Department for Education and Skills (DfES) and managed by the British Educational and Communications Technology Agency (Becta). The team comprised: Colin Harrison (Project Director), Tony Fisher, Kaye Haw, Eric Lunzer (University of Nottingham); Peter Scrimshaw (Co-Director) and Cathy Lewin (Open University); and Bridget Somekh (Co-Director) and Diane Mavers (Manchester Metropolitan University).

Also included are non-funded visits to schools, and texts made by the children of colleagues and extended family.

Extract from *Oxford Very First Dictionary* compiled by Clare Kirtley, illustrated by Georgie Birkett (OUP 2007), copyright © Oxford University Press 1999, reprinted by permission of Oxford University Press.

THANKS

I would like to express my thanks to the people who generously allowed me to study the texts appearing in this book, and those who have been formative of my thinking. Thanks to the project directors Colin Harrison and Bridget Somekh, and to the evaluation funders, for allowing me to undertake secondary analysis of materials gathered during my work as a researcher, where broader project designs provide a context for interpreting the children's texts and text making. I am grateful to the Oracle Education Foundation for consent to write about materials gathered online from ThinkQuest (http://www.thinkquest.org) and to GridClub (www.gridclub.com) - Grid Learning Limited. My particular thanks go to the children, and to their parents / carers, for their consent. I am also grateful to the head teachers who allowed me to visit their schools, and to the teachers who welcomed me into their classrooms. It was the seminal book *Before Writing: Rethinking the Paths to Literacy* by Gunther Kress that resonated with my experience of children's text making as a class teacher and as a researcher. With thanks to Gunther for his inspiration and guidance, and for continuing conversations over coffee in the park. I apologize if, immersed in this way of seeing the world, I have at any point failed to make due reference to his work. I am especially grateful to Bridget Somekh, always generous, who introduced me to the world of research, included me fully in all aspects of evaluation projects, encouraged me to pursue my own interests and gave me numerous opportunities to present my work. Without her, I would not be where I am now. My thanks are also extended to Ben Holtzman and Max Novick at Routledge for their support and patience, and to Michael Watters for all his help with copy editing.

EARLIER PUBLICATIONS

Some of the materials appearing in this book draw on earlier publications:

Mavers, D. (2009) 'Student text-making as semiotic work', *Journal of Early Childhood Literacy*, 9(2): 141–155.

Mavers, D. (2007) 'Semiotic resourcefulness: a young child's email exchange as design', *Journal of Early Childhood Literacy*, 7(2): 155–176.

Mavers, D. (2003) 'Communicating meanings through image composition, spatial arrangement and links in primary school student mind maps', in C. Jewitt and G. Kress (eds.), *Multimodal Literacy* (pp. 19–33), New York: Peter Lang.

1   A Lens on the Unremarkable

The unremarkable is actually remarkable. Much of children's everyday text making is apparently unexceptional: a swift drawing dashed off in a few moments, a routine classroom exercise, exchanging messages, copying from the class whiteboard. Yet, viewed through a certain lens, what children do as a matter of course becomes surprising. Ordinariness masks richness and complexity, routine features that pass by largely unnoticed are not at all trivial and commonplace 'errors', even if not overlooked, are replete with meaningfulness. What might appear mundane, effortless, mistaken, even uninteresting, turns out to be intriguing.

The quintessence of ordinariness, a text made at home by Shakira (age 6 years) epitomizes the remarkable in the unremarkable (Figure 1.1). Her drawings of frontally-oriented people are readily recognizable, but why are they different sizes? On the enlarged hands, Shakira included palm lines or traces of bones, but elsewhere she omitted other details such as the colour, texture and style of clothing, and background. Why did she do this? Arms are omitted on the smaller figure, even though Shakira knew how to draw them (see also Cox, 1992: 41–42; Golomb, 1974: 104; Goodnow, 1977: 65). Is this a mistake? Where the proportions of drawing do not match those of the actual world and where certain features are not incorportaed, a possible inference is deficiency: either mistakenness in how children see the world or immaturity in their drawing skills. Could there be an alternative explanation? The caption—'Mum is my Hirow (Hero) Br Br (Barbara) too'—might raise a smile, but what about the 'incorrect' spellings and omission of punctuation marks? Is this inability or immaturity, or can it be seen in a different way? Yet other questions arise. Why did Shakira choose the present tense? Why did she position her writing one block above the other, and below the drawing of her mother? Why does 'Hirow' reside in writing rather than drawing? She drew and wrote with green glitter pen and trimmed the sheet with chopped cuts to remove extraneous paper. Is this meaningful? An entirely everyday text such as this raises issues central to investigation of the unremarkable. What is and is not noticed, who notices, and why?

Figure 1.1   'Mum is my Hirow' (Shakira).

THE IDEOLOGY OF THE LENS

Whilst by no means denying that children develop physically and that they learn increasingly about the world and being in the world, the dominant view that they progress from asociality to sociality, from simplicity to complexity, from irrationality to rationality and from incompetence to competence has proven 'extraordinarily resistant to criticism' (Prout and James, 1997: 22). This is only one step away from slippage into seeing children as deficient. Of course, they do not have adults' breadth of social experience, and they have many years of school education ahead of them. Even so, discourses of inadequacy, shortcoming and ignorance focus on what children cannot do. Viewing them as in need of improvement, correction or 'filling up' distracts attention from the sophistication of what they can do and the range of what they do know.

Regarding children as social agents shifts the focus. It takes seriously their 'work' as they participate in the environments in which they find themselves. Social roles, relationships and interactions are generated in the dynamism of people engaging with one another, and this includes children. Of course, young people's lives are shaped and constrained, even determined, by adults. Yet, as they participate in everyday social activities—whether interacting around the kitchen table, working in the classroom, playing in the park, shopping, or whatever else—what goes on is not just a case of social determinism. Children frame, interpret and respond. Doing what is expected of them takes social and semiotic effort as they figure out what is needed on this occasion. Children are not merely compliant respondents. Their very engagement as they weigh up, abide by, oppose and negotiate exchange with others both sustains, reproduces and challenges existing discourses and practices. The well-established and highly particularized rules and social relations of school construct one such space where young people both conform and contest. Children act upon the powerful ideologies of what is done and how (Hutchby and Moran-Ellis, 1998; James, Jenks and Prout, 1998; Prout and James, 1997). This marks a shift from socialization to disposition, from 'being done to' to participation.

Common parlance, the well-established term 'acquisition' (e.g. 'language acquisition', 'knowledge acquisition', 'skills acquisition') implies that children learn through osmosis, just as the pedagogic notion of 'delivery' presupposes largely uninterrupted 'reception'. The notions of transmission and assimilation background agency, with an attendant positioning of children as absorbers of knowledge and experience. An alternative is that learning requires semiotic effort. Something is attended to, be it a new-born baby recognizing the reaching out of a hand, a preschooler working out the rules of tense or plurality (e.g. 'I goed', 'the feets'), a beginning reader making sense of the shapes of script or a school scientist puzzling over the use of arrows to show magnetic force. An alternative to passivity is engagement and 'work'.

Representation and communication are never ideologically neutral (Halliday, 1978; Hodge and Kress, 1988; Lemke, 1990). What and how children draw and write are framed by what is valued, and what is valued in one social environment might be denigrated, ignored or reconfigured in another. This shapes what they are asked, expected or choose to do, how their efforts are received and how their texts are evaluated. The ideology of the lens—how texts are looked at—frames what is recognized. This is highly political because what is acknowledged shapes how young people are positioned, whether as social agents or as developmentally deficient, or whatever else. Even from the youngest age, how children are seen and how they come to see themselves as text makers are formative of their dispositions and identities. Societal and educational discourses and practices have far reaching implications not only for what it means to be literate, and more broadly an assured text maker, but also for citizenship and social justice.

A LENS ON THE UNREMARKABLE IN CHILDREN'S DRAWING AND WRITING

The so-called 'scribble' produced by very young children was formerly—and sometimes still is—considered to be motor action undertaken and

enjoyed for its own sake, 'chaotic' and devoid of representational intentionality (Matthews, 1999: 4), even 'meaningless'. This has led to the commonly held view that their drawings are deficient. More recent research
shows that intense multidirectional lines, shading of areas or 'patches'
can represent the solidity of people, animals or make-believe characters
(Buckham, 1994: 134–137) or inanimate objects (Matthews, 1999: 34).
Different kinds of marks (looped and single lines or 'slashes' and zigzags)
can show existence, number and location, and body parts may be represented discretely rather than connected (Lancaster, 2007; Wolf and Perry,
1988: 20). Pre-schoolers' representations can depict sensations such as
a hurting knee or tactility such as the feel of a blanket (Brittain, 1979:
30, 33). It is not that this is wrong. Even if unlike the drawing of older
children, these are marks of meaning, neither haphazard nor accidental,
but 'principled' (a term I borrow from Gunther Kress here and throughout the book). In order to show the defining attributes of people, animals
and objects, a common feature of early drawing is that children may not
restrict themselves to one angle only. It is not that representations with
multiple viewpoints are any less sophisticated than a single perspective,
or that there is an historical or developmental progression from one to the
other (see also Cox, 2005; Golomb, 1999). In drawing without one fixed
point of view, such as a family around the dining table (Matthews, 1999:
84–93), a friend on the other side of the street (Lowenfeld and Brittain,
1987: 269) or children in a circle enacting a playground rhyme (Cox,
1992: 137), angle is a semiotic resource that provides the potential for
making certain meanings.

What if what is commonly assumed to be mistaken is looked at
again? As 4-year-olds moved between writing-like squiggles and meticulously formed lettering, this was not a case of a linear progression from
'scribble' to 'proper writing' (Kenner, 2000b: 254–264), or 'reverting'
to immaturity. Rather, their representations were shaped by purpose.
Fluent inscription of a linear succession of circular shapes was an act
of writerly performance, with the visual appearance of continuousness
being deemed apt for a story and horizontal completion of a grid-like
structure being well suited to signifying a class register. On the other
hand, careful attention to the detail of the Arabic script was a way of
demonstrating seriousness in engaging with alphabetic form. As they
observe and participate in text-making activities, children gain access
to and make meaning with an ever-widening range of resources. This
shifts the focus to which resources children have available to them and
how they deploy them at their discretion within the framing of specific
activities.

Literacy is highly valued in many contemporary societies. Spelling—
where the script is alphabetic—maintains a key place in contemporary
policy, curriculum, teaching and assessment. We want children to be able

to spell competently, because this equips them with the resources to participate confidently in different social domains. As they learn the rules and irregularities of Standard English spelling, they do not always 'get it right'. Shakira wrote 'Hirow' instead of 'hero' and 'BrBr' instead of 'Barbara' (Figure 1.1). How is this to be understood and handled? One response is to say that it is a good attempt for a child of this age, but that some of the spellings are plain wrong and will be rectified in time, with instruction, correction and practice. Alternatively, features that might be judged inaccurate can be seen as being replete with resourcefulness. Where children are taught to identify phonemes and to 'build' words using phonics, Shakira's spellings represent a principled effort to transcribe the sounds of speech. Inadequacy is replaced by resourcefulness and agency. Even so, teachers are responsible for supporting children towards what is valued educationally as set out in the requirements of the curriculum, which includes learning to spell correctly. This raises questions around how learning opportunities are designed and how children's efforts are responded to. The desired outcome remains educationally and societally valued, but the process of getting there comes to the fore.

Over the course of their schooling, children learn to create a range of genres: stories, poems, reports, lists, instructions and so on. As they move between different subjects of the curriculum, learning to interpret and represent graphically the specialized knowledge of each subject area according to its particular and shared representational conventions is not without challenge (Gee, 2003; Unsworth, 2001). The co-presence of narrative, map and game in the same text (Barrs, 1988; Pahl, 2001) might be judged as flawed. In certain contexts, this would be the case. Made at home as part of self-generated activities, such texts may be generically mixed, but are they a muddle? As children transport representational resources between school and home, they make the most of familiar and newly discovered forms in their shaping of meaning. They also integrate features of contemporary popular culture such as characters and events from digital games, comics, cartoons and films (e.g. Dyson, 2008; Marsh and Millard, 2000) in ways that do not necessarily cohere with formal genres. Viewed not as deficiency but as resourcefulness, this demonstrates initiative as children make the most of what is to hand in investigating forms and structures, and discourses and genres. It is important that children learn to create texts that conform to convention. Given the space to explore and experiment, we see the inventiveness, originality and ingenuity of their drawing and writing.

Change has been intense in recent times, with upheavals on an unprecedented and unforeseen scale. Stabilities in finance, employment, national and global politics and social relationships have been undone in quite unanticipated ways. Along with this, text-making practices unthought of fifty years ago have become commonplace and un-extraordinary. With increasing affordability of, and access to, an ever-widening range of digital technologies in many contemporary societies, children play video games, surf the web, shop online, download music, exchange online messages, blog, make web pages, and post photographs and movies (Carrington, 2005; Downes, 2002; Facer, 2003; Holloway and Valentine, 2003; Knobel, 2006; Livingstone and Bovill, 2001). Commonplace and un-extraordinary, these forms of, and practices in, authorship, dissemination and interaction have transformed communicational possibilities, and are redefining literacy (Carrington, 2004; Lankshear and Knobel, 2003). Indeed, current debate questions whether 'digital literacy' is sufficient to account for expanding multimodal forms of text making.

A LENS FOR INVESTIGATING CHILDREN'S DRAWING AND WRITING

Social semiotics is concerned with signs, sign making and sign makers. The Swiss linguist Ferdinand de Saussure, one of the founders of semiotics, proposed that a sign is a 'double entity' comprising a signifier and a signified (Saussure, 1966: 65). In his study of the spoken sounds of Indo-European languages, this duality, he argues, does not consist of a naming word corresponding to the thing it names but respectively to a 'sound-image' produced physically and a 'concept' constructed in the mind: the physiological and the psychological (ibid.: 66). Beyond the signifiers of speech that interested Saussure, the social semiotic notion of 'resource' embraces all modes of representation and communication (e.g. writing, drawing, gesture, gaze, dress, etc.). Sign making is embodied, not just 'mindful'. Replacement of 'concept' with 'meaning' broadens the scope of what can be signified to include, for example, the affective, attitudes and perspectives—and the social. A coherent theoretical and analytical framework unrestricted to any one mode provides a means for examining representation and communication irrespective of what it is.

For the most part, children's writing and drawing have been studied separately, the former mainly by language and literacy specialists, and the latter largely by developmental and cognitive psychologists, and art educators. As a consequence, much is known about writing and drawing discretely. Their co-presence in children's text making has been by no means ignored in research. With the recent emergence of multimodality as a domain of inquiry, writing and drawing have been examined as inter-semiotic rather merely co-present, with implications for design, the representation of knowledge and the construction of identity (e.g. Bearne, 2003; Mavers, 2009; Pahl, 2004). Multimodal texts are ensembles made with the resources of more than one mode. Settling on whether writing or drawing is best suited to purpose demands resolutions with regard to the distribution of meanings and the relationships between them.

At first sight, different kinds of graphic texts—a drawing, copying from a picture dictionary, digital exchange—appear to have little in common. They entail different modes of representation, different media, different identities, different purposes, different environments, and no doubt other things too. If representation is taken to consist of form and meaning (or 'sign') then certain questions can be asked irrespective of what it is. How are signs made in a range of ways? Why was this mode chosen for this sign making? What would have been the consequences of choosing a different mode? Can the same meaning be expressed in different ways, or are certain meanings exclusive to either writing or drawing? As graphic forms of representation, are any resources shared? Where is the semiotic load? What has been put with what? What relationships have been constructed between modes? In their handling of a variety of resources in their shaping of meaning, what does this imply about children as makers of texts?

In investigating the unremarkable features of children's drawing and writing as agentive design, a theory of representation must be able to offer a means of accounting for the routine and commonplace, including 'errors', as investment of 'work'. It was Saussure's view that the relationship between signifier (*signifiant*) and signified (*signifié*) in a word sign is generally arbitrary in the sense that the sounds of speech bear no relation to what the thing being referred to is (Saussure, 1966: 67, 73). Notwithstanding the etymology of word roots, of which children are unlikely to be aware, there appears to be some sense in the contention that the marks of writing bear no visual relation to the actual things they represent. This, however, is an observation on the extent to which the form of a signifier has 'resemblance' to that which it signifies. What if the focus shifts to semiotic (sign-making) processes? A social semiotic approach maintains that people do not use ready-made signs; they make them (Kress, 1993, 1997). This perspective challenges the commonly held view that culturally developed and socially enforced codes are acquired and applied. In an entirely ordinary process, signs are constantly made afresh as composites of form (or signifier) and meaning (or signified). Even though the sign maker produces meaning with well-acknowledged and readily available representational resources, the sign that is made is always semiotically 'new' (The New London Group, 2000). The notion of agentive sign making within the regularities of socially and culturally shaped discourses, genres and practices is ideologically significant because it has implications for how text making and text makers are understood. Within the framing of purpose and social relations, people have and exercise choice in their shaping of meaning. What children draw and write is not coded, but principled.

The meaning potentialities of representational and communicational resources are shaped by semiotic provenance. A semiotic resource bears the social and cultural history of innumerable occasions when it has been chosen for sign making, and this shapes its ongoing suitability. Through sometimes long and sometimes more recently established practices, patterns in how meanings are made with available resources are regularities that are sustained by power and convention. Culturally shaped and made available socially—and particularized in the practices of different social groups—meanings associated with the signifiers of writing and drawing are, on the whole, broadly stable, and this is what enables shared understanding. Meaning is constrained within certain parameters. The phrase 'Mum is my Hirow', for example, locks out a whole plethora of meanings, and is inclusive of others. Other forms are more open. Kneeling backwards on a public transport seat, a young child pressed the tip of his right index finger into the centre of a brightly coloured outline of a square which formed part of the patterning of the fabric covering. Absorbed and without recourse to the adults accompanying him who were deeply engaged in conversation, he proceeded to inspect the seat cover meticulously, systematically prodding the centre of each shape. On completion, he pressed the squares in a patterned sequence, making a different beeping sound for each by adjusting the length and pitch of his articulations. The boy then turned to his mother and announced, 'It's a robot.' At that moment, the form of outline shapes was suggestive to him of digital buttons. At another time, they might evoke something else. Representational and communicational forms have semiotic histories that render them redolent of certain socially and culturally habituated meanings and exclusive to or inhibiting of others. This tempers a division between form and meaning. Socially available signifying resources are suggestive of meaning because of their semiotic provenance; there are regularized ways in which meanings are made with them. On the other hand, people make meaning in a variety of ways. It follows that individuality and sociality are entirely interrelated. Children are agentive within the framing of socially sedimented regularities.

The term 'text' derives from the Latin *textus* meaning 'a weave'. Text making is the interweaving of forms and meanings in design and production, and the material instantiation of text is the sum of its semiotic features.

'A text is 'what is meant', selected from the total set of options that constitute what can be meant. In other words, text can be defined as actualized meaning potential' (Halliday, 1978: 109).

Entirely ordinary, texts are orchestrated in combinations of choices. What is drawn or written is an assemblage that represents a series of selections. Every selection is relational. Choices are made with reference to, and have consequences for, other choices: with a view to those already made, relative to those being made and in anticipation of those yet to be made. In the shaping of meaning with the resources to hand, this demands consideration of possibilities, decision making, planning and organization. Infinite variations are made possible by the numerous ways in which forms and meanings can be deployed and related in the interweaving of *textus*.

Drawing and writing are forms of text making. Making is not just doing; it is principled social action. When they draw and write, children engage in the interrelated 'work' of interpretation, evaluation, design and production. Framed by what it is that is being done, for whom and with whom, they weigh up the characteristics of the environment. Relations of power shift; practices vary; subject matter is diverse. In the dynamism of fast-moving events and interactions with others, appraisal and reappraisal are ongoing. Children's interpretations of these complexities constitute the ground for their text making. Always adaptive, always an alignment to the here and now, 'design' (Kress, 2000; Kress and Van Leeuwen, 2001: 45–65) is the shaping of meaning in choosing the resources deemed apt to the particular framing (even if that framing is self imposed). It involves assessment of what is needed, consideration of alternatives, making judgements, forward planning, resolving difficulties and reaching solutions. Text makers are faced with a whole raft of questions. What is it that I wish to express? Who is this for? What must be included and what can be omitted? What is a suitable means of expression? What should go with what? In attending to the interrelationship between the 'what', the 'why', the 'who for' and the 'how', the text maker takes account of subject matter, the person or people for whom the text is intended and the representational modes and media available. People realize their designs as material entities in the physical act of production. Imagined and then made materially (if sometimes produced and then interpreted and integrated into the design), the resulting artefact represents the text maker's semiotic settling on resource and meaning at that moment in time. Drawing and writing realize what the maker considered apt to this occasion, in response to purpose, audience and aesthetics, and within the possibilities and constraints of the environment.

Children select and combine resources in their shaping of meaning, not randomly, but in ways that are principled (Kress, 1997). Text making demands 'semiotic work'—a term I borrow from Gunther Kress (2010) here and throughout the book. Semiotic work is not just activity; it is principled engagement with and in the shaping of meaning. This shifts the focus from innateness, acquisition and competence to effortful making. The work of drawing and writing entails a semiotic worker (with a working identity) and semiotic work to be done (discursively and generically framed representation or communication) with certain means (the semiotic resources available to the individual) and in a particular environment (with certain social practices). Taking seriously the various features of the texts children make, whatever they are and however ordinary, respects the semiotic effort they commit to their drawing and writing. Inadequacy and deficit give way to agency and 'work'.

DIRECTING THE LENS

Not all kinds of texts are equally valued, even noticed. A child in a Reception class (4- and 5-year-olds) 'copied' with intense concentration and systematic searching images from a non-fiction book. His investment of effort as he engaged in this self-initiated task resulted in a text that consisted of 'just' a series of pencil marks arranged vertically down the centre of the page, apparently 'nothing'. It was later gathered without acknowledgement. What 'work' is entailed in remaking one text as another? Furthermore, some features of text are highly valued, whilst others are commonly deemed less significant and, whilst not without interest, are not given equal consideration. This creates hierarchies in what is attended to, with some aspects more readily recognized and some barely acknowledged at all. As a consequence, more is known about meaning making with some resources than others, for example the lexis and grammar of writing as against how it is arranged in the space of the graphic surface, or the viewpoints and occlusion of drawing as against its material realization. This distracts attention from some of the attributes of texts made by children. If only certain features are recognized and others are backgrounded, construed as meaningless, even disregarded because they lie beyond that which is commonly valued, the semiotic plenitude of text is overlooked.

What can we learn about children's text making if what is generally discounted is examined with seriousness? What if ordinariness and 'imperfection' are looked at again? If attention is given to what children can do rather what they cannot, what can we learn about their text making? If there is a temporary bracketing of competence, ability and attainment and a foregrounding of interpretation, participation and work, what insights can this provide? A lens that brings into focus agency, purpose and principles is not romanticism or sentimentalism, nor is it mere celebration. Rather, it seeks to recognize the semiotic work children invest in their text making. Nor does this automatically suggest the obverse, namely that parents, educators and researchers do not recognize and value what youngsters do. With the greatest respect for teachers committed to children's education, the argument developed in this book does not underestimate or undermine admirable pedagogic practice, sometimes in challenging contexts. Rather, it aims to unsettle what might be taken for granted, and to open up debate.

This book investigates a variety of ways in which children shape meaning in the semiotic work of their drawing and writing, and seeks to understand text making from the perspective of the child acting seriously in the world. Children are prolific makers of a range of texts. As they go about their everyday lives, they draw and write for a multiplicity of surprisingly diverse, and not mutually exclusive, purposes: to solve problems, to demonstrate learning, to explore ideas and feelings, to create imagined worlds, to greet, to plan, to document their experiences, to communicate with others, and so on. Subject matter is wide ranging, and includes places they have visited, objects or living things that intrigue them, things they have done, people they care about, issues that concern them, curricular entities and more besides. Made for and given to an assortment of people—family, carers, friends, teachers, themselves—audiences shift. Chapter 2 investigates the routine practice of copying—widely disparaged as 'a waste of time'—as a process of re-production, redesign and recontextualization. Examination of ordinariness in Chapter 3 focuses on features of text that pass by largely unacknowledged, meanings made in processes of production and how children notice the semiotic potentialities of media. Chapter 4 explores the principled semiotic work entailed in apparent 'errors', how 'getting it wrong' may actually be 'getting it right' and how 'mistakes' are handled in different social environments. In Chapter 5, texts that might appear at first sight to be 'just a mess' turn out not to be a disorderly confusion after all, and shorthand and repetition emerge as signs of sophistication rather than shortfall. Adopting the notion of frames around classroom text making, Chapter 6 investigates how semiosis becomes fixed as a material entity, even if only momentarily, and how 'just' brief and fleeting text making entails semiotic work. Chapter 7 examines how remaking one text as another, largely unacknowledged in research and practice, entails handling complex shifts in form and meaning. In noticing the unnoticed and accounting for the discounted, Chapter 8 reflects on ideologies of the unremarkable, with particular respect to recognition, change, diversity and flexibility in fostering positive semiotic dispositions.

2 'Copying'

Existing texts can provide a source for text making. Children engage with materials found in storybooks, comics, non-fiction resources, on the web, and so on, and produce something in response. Where the resulting text is identical to or very like the original, this would generally be viewed as copying. Deemed to be 'nothing' because it is mere replication, copying is unworthy of attention. Considered ethically 'wrong' or educationally unacceptable, the very act of investigation of itself acknowledges that it goes on. Albeit founded on well-established societal principles and well-substantiated educational concerns, these discourses have held back study of children's 'copying' as something that warrants serious attention. Is copying 'just' replication? What if it is examined as semiotic work?

IDEOLOGIES OF COPYING

Like all text making, copying is ideologically framed. The boundaries of what is and is not acceptable are specific to socially, culturally and historically located values and beliefs. Ideologies shift. In Japan, copying is a feature of certain cultural practices, including performance rituals, tea making and calligraphy (Cox, 2008). Copywriting in Victorian England (1837–1901) occupied a substantial proportion of the school curriculum. Copperplate was highly valued, whilst creative writing was not deemed essential for children whose futures lay in coalmines, cotton mills and the manufacture of ships and trains. Amongst art educators, particularly between the 1950s and 1970s, the issue of copying was highly contentious and attracted sustained debate. Opponents condemned its detrimental effects on children's 'natural' self-expression, arguing that it stunts creativity and 'mental growth' and promotes dependency, whilst supporters saw it as an interpretive process and a way of developing technique (Duncum, 1989).

Copying is widely and decisively denigrated in many schools in contemporary England. And yet, more or less recognized, it goes on. Pedagogically, it is denounced as a low-level activity that keeps children busy, that lacks intellectual challenge, and that thwarts imagination and creativity. The very mention of the term induces suspicion. Across a handful of exploratory visits to schools, broaching this topic proved delicate and was met with affront. Teachers and senior managers were surprised and mildly insulted that its occurrence could even be imagined, and the denial 'we don't copy in our school' was without exception. Children shared this discourse. Even below the age of formal schooling, copying another child's writing or drawing was considered an offence and a justified reason for indignation and complaint. Airing a more positive view, 8-year-old Leona's reflection on the practice of sharing curricular work—'In class, we don't think of copying as copying (.) we think of copying as like just borrowing ideas'—was immediately countered by the comment 'Borrowing their ideas (..) Miss says that to make us feel better.' Educational concerns are with the quality of learning, indeed whether any learning has taken place. Copying through student choice is commonly deemed to be a failure to engage 'properly' with subject matter as a consequence of an inability to understand challenging materials (Wray and Lewis, 1997: 152), and, at worst, laziness. With older students, ethical concerns around plagiarism with its undertones of cheating and stealing introduce covertness, and even induce moral panic. Access to innumerable materials in print and on the web can make its occurrence difficult to trace, with related concerns around getting good marks without putting in the required intellectual effort.

Discourses associated with practices in school are not necessarily sustained in other social environments. Contemporary forms of digital text making entail widespread and entirely commonplace practices in 'remixing' materials. The same photographs appear in different web pages advertising Mozart tourist attractions and memorabilia (Ventola, 2006). In order to keep up with the fast-moving pace of synchronous written exchange in chat, copying and pasting is a device used to sustain the momentum of response. You-Tubers copy and paste extracts of video footage to summarize topic streams, with selections and assemblages creating new texts (Adami, 2009). Although images and chunks of writing, even whole soundtracks, are shared, 'mashups' are not seen as copies but as (re)designs that create new meanings (e.g. pastiches, parodies, ironies).

Unlike handmade texts, in copying and pasting on the computer the act is humanly performed but the processing is digital. Notwithstanding screen resolution, form is remade exactly and automatically. A web page created and published by Nicola (age 9 years), like many others in the child-only environment where it was produced, consisted almost entirely of images copied and pasted from the web. Was this 'just messing around'? From the countless images available (with adequate search skills), Nicola had selected an animated image which she placed in the position normally allocated to the title at the top centre of the screen. From a thin, curved line of coloured balls that cascaded downwards, individual balls rolled from side to side, bounced and made circular movements. Animations were said to 'make it fun' and to be associated with attracting attention, stimulating interest and sustaining engagement:

'Moving pictures are more attractive because if they're just still it looks a bit boring (..) but when they're moving around and things like that it makes you feel ha (.) jolly (..) and it makes you feel like you want to move onto things and see what other pictures are there.'

The significance of this choice became apparent in relation to what appeared below: seven photographs of Nicola's favourite football star. In selecting certain images—and, by default, rejecting others—these were not random choices. They captured different facets of the celebrity's life (his professional role as a footballer, relaxing in his leisure time, spending time with his family), exhibited him in a variety of poses (jogging, standing to attention, sitting), included different moods (smiling, serious, proud, determined, protective), showed different appearances (football kit, leisurewear, hat, glasses) and included different types of shots (full body, head and upper body, head and shoulders; frontal and profile). Apparently self-explanatory, no labelling was supplied. Visitors to Nicola's web page were expected to recognize this as a themed collection. Meaningfulness also resided in her design of layout; she manipulated the size of the images and arranged their positioning. Largest and centrally placed, the star was foregrounded in the role he is famous for: in action on the pitch—full length, frontal and jogging. Towards the bottom of the screen, she had pasted an animated line drawing of a spinning heart. Wordless, this represented her affective response at a glance. Scrolling down, a relatively diminutive written link led to Nicola's summary of the latest news about the star's role in his league and national team, injury details and his personal life. This was not meaningless copying and pasting. Nicola selected and presented existing images of varying online provenance for a new purpose.

A default deficit view that copying is 'nothing', that it does not require 'work', does not cohere with practices in digital environments such as this. It was not the case that copying and pasting a collection of images was 'just messing around'. On the contrary, it was intensely purposeful. Publishing a web page that was suited to the online community for which it was designed required recognition of existing practices in order to participate in a way that was acceptable, thereby validating membership, establishing identity and prompting communicational interaction. Making the web page was not at all haphazard, nor was it without effort. It required searching, navigation, selection, arrangement, rescaling, and so on. Pedagogic concerns about copying and pasting materials on the computer create a tension between widely accepted forms of and practices in digital text making beyond school, and those in school.

RE-PRODUCTION

Copying is generally thought of as exact and unvarying replication. Looking below the surface begins to challenge this assumption. With contemporary equipment such as photocopiers and scanners, a copy is apparently identical to its original. Each line and shape is reproduced with exactness. Even so, a consequence of the remediating process is that materiality is not necessarily shared. The original graphic surface is replaced by the texture, weight and shade of the 'destination' paper or by pixels on a screen. Indentations made by pressing down heavily can no longer be felt, and marks made in erasing or creasing may become difficult to make out. Original substances are lost. For example, not only is the tactility of wax crayon absent in scanning or photocopying, but also its sheen and the changing effects of refracted light (see Figure 7.2a). Hues may not be identical, or may be replaced by grey-scale. Size may be rescaled, such as maps originally made on large sheets of A3 paper (see Chapter 5). Even digitally copied texts are not an exact replication. This casts into doubt what a copy actually is.

A social semiotic perspective holds that all signs—composites of form (a signifier resource) and meaning (that which is signified)—are agentively made (Kress, 1997). Taking the view that copying is 'mindless' replication, that it is entirely mechanical, would entail switching off the dynamic processes of sign making. Is agency severed in copying? If the theoretical principle of agentive sign making is maintained, then it must hold irrespective of the task being undertaken. With this perspective, signs are not transported wholesale. Copying is a relational process where an existing material entity is interpreted and then remade as a different material entity. As both text interpreter and text producer, the 'copier' handles form and meaning in two sites. The source text consists of a collection of signifiers. These become signs in the act of interpretation as meanings are connected with the forms that are given. Making the copy is also a process of sign making. The 'copier' connects form and meaning in the production of the copy. This shifts the focus to the kinds of semiotic work that copying entails.

A commonly held view is that it is educationally acceptable for young children to copy letters and numbers because they are 'just' learning to re-produce form and meaning comes later. From a social semiotic perspective, all representation is sign making, and all sign making entails processes of connecting form and meaning or meaning and form. Young children can become absorbed in copying their names (Pahl, 1999: 60–69), images on packaging and in books (Gardner, 1980: 100–112, 192–198; Kress, 1997: 54), letters from alphabet charts and phrases they have dictated. What is going on here? Experimentation provides opportunities to explore 'what happens if'. As children 'play' with signifier resources, they investigate how different marks have different effects. This fascination is a semiotic inquiry into the relationship between form and meaning. Re-production may also aim towards 'getting it right'. In part, this is an endeavour to recreate for themselves texts that are established, recognized and valued, and that will have currency in everyday life.

Inside and filling the available space of the front and back covers of a biography are three consecutive attempts at a mathematical problem, each succeeded by a 'copy' made by a younger brother. The circumstances in which this was undertaken are lost. It may be that choice of an illicit, unlikely-to-be-discovered place was a consequence of paper being scarce, or perhaps inscription of their father's name and two addresses (the former crossed out) legitimized writing in this hardback book. At this age, Tim would not have known how to set out or perform long multiplication such as this. His 'copying' was perhaps borne of an interest in inscriptions or maybe a desire to emulate the 'work' done by an older sister. Exhaustive in his attention to each graphic component, his re-production of line, conjoining, shape, size, length, directionality, arrangement and positioning—sometimes mirrored or upturned—is suggestive of the demands of the endeavour (Figure 2.1). So what about the lowest component? To a more experienced mathematician, the 'answer' of the original would be interpreted in the context of the problem as a whole, with the downward stroke preceding the '5' and the forward slash inside its lower curve suspended as 'mistakes'. For a young child seeking to re-produce form, every mark is significant. Tim's 'copy' is not at all random, but represents serious attention to form. As one text is remade into another, it can be argued that there is no such thing as a copy because copying is an agentive process of remaking afresh.

As evidence of having engaged with and understood what they have read, children are often exhorted by teachers to 'write it in your own words'. In this more extensive kind of redesign, certain shared signifying features would be expected such as words and groups of words, with the proportion of similarity or sameness—the relative weighting of copied and not-copied items—being a measure of what is and is not acceptable. As signifiers are common property, their recurrence is ongoing (see also Collerson, 1986; The New London Group, 2000). It is their appearance in configurations sufficiently different from the source text that assures teachers of the re-expression of meaning, whilst a fair degree of similarity slips into the 'danger area' of copying. A copy is deemed to be a copy when the product is like the source that was its origin in fundamental ways; it is characterized by similarity, even sameness to the original. It follows that what copying is is tied up with constancy of signifying features. Where the copy is in many respects closely identical to the original, a large proportion of signifiers is shared. These material forms can be tracked, shown and described. Tracing meaning is more slippery. Where a signifier is identical to the original (e.g. a word, a punctuation mark, a shape, positioning), the meaning that has been made of and with it may be difficult to recover, even irrecoverable. It is this that makes copying worrying for educators.

Once inscriptional forms are established and children have sufficient resources to write and draw with some degree of independence, a concern with copying is that form may be re-produced without sufficient engagement with subject matter. Sonita's 'copy' is perhaps the closest to her teacher's in a class set of 27 children aged between 9 and 10 years (Figure 2.2a, b). The 'content' was elicited from and negotiated with the class, and

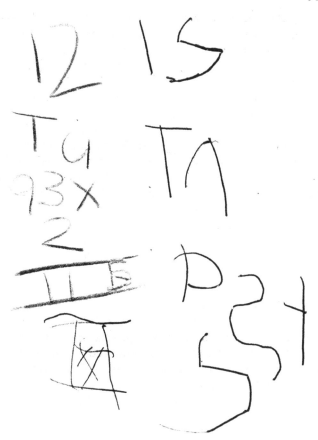

Figure 2.1   'Copy' of long multiplication (Tim).

then recorded by the teacher in real time on a piece of paper placed on the class visualiser (a digital display technology). Apart from three minor variations (omission of underlining and substitution of one capital letter for lower case in the title, plus a crossing out half way down the page), this is remarkably close to the source text in terms of wording, layout, punctuation, and even handwriting. The contention that this makes recovering meaning problematic is not unsubstantiated. A pressing question is what the 'copier' was attending to. Meaning was made of something—but of what? This can be difficult to trace. If a signifier in the copy is identical to that of the source text, the meaning(s) made of and with it may be inaccessible from the copy alone. Where copying is done independently and in oral silence, as in this case, clues in simultaneous interactions are unavailable. From the 'copy' alone, we cannot second-guess Sonita's interpretation of the meanings of written words and groupings of words. What we can be sure of is that she gave very careful attention to the graphic entity—the lettering, presentation, punctuation and arrangement of the text—otherwise she could not have re-produced it with such precision. Her subscripted prediction, which was not copied, is not at all indiscriminate. It repeats certain lexical items ('amount', 'water', 'change') and is semantically related ('go down' links with 'evaporated' and 'centemeters (centimetres)' connects with 'unit of measurement'). There is semiotic connectedness between the more constrained copied component and the more open addition.

The act of production can provide certain insights into meaning making. In the temporality of the process of making a copy, interpretation precedes material production, and this sequence can be tracked. The site of the source text in manual copying—whether at a distance such as on the class board or screen, or in a book positioned nearby on the table—demands that attention is shifted between two locations. The order in which graphic items and components of these items are re-produced may be significant. Children 'copied' the writing of a dictionary extract first (see below). When they came to the spatiality of drawing, there was choice in where to begin. Nabil did his lion's head first (Figure 2.4c), whereas Miguel started at the tip of the upright tail (Figure 2.4d), an indication not of randomness, but of their immediate interests, and of prior planning. Writing offers less scope for choice because of its linearity; the copier starts at the beginning of the section to be copied and proceeds in a sequential order. Chunking blocks of writing, first interpreted and then re-produced, requires that decisions are made about the amount of text that can and will be handled in one 'go'. Frequency and duration of reference back to the original source text are purported to be indicators of memory capacity (Mahalski, 1995: 10). As Emil 'copied' the third condition of a fair test, he looked up at the teacher's

Fair Test – Evaporation

What we will observe: How much water evaporated.

We will change: the place we put our sample.

We will keep the same: The type of liquid
Amount of liquid
Container
Same person. measuring.
Same unit of measurement

My prediction:

2.2a   The teacher's original.

writing displayed on the class screen 15 times over a period of 1 minute 46 seconds, writing either one or two words after each glance (Figure 2.2d).

Precision in copying is generally judged by likeness to the original. 'Inaccuracies' in copied writing are commonly deemed to be a consequence of

2.2b   Sonita's 'copy'.

2.2c   Emil's 'copy'.

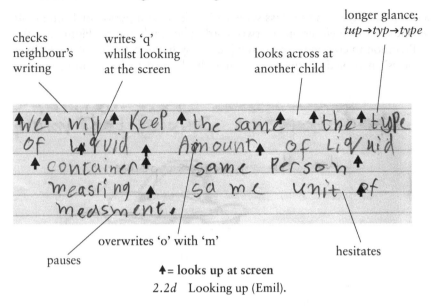

checks neighbour's writing

writes 'q' whilst looking at the screen

looks across at another child

longer glance; *tup→typ→type*

overwrites 'o' with 'm'

pauses

hesitates

✦ = looks up at screen

2.2d   Looking up (Emil).

Figure 2.2   'Copying' from the class screen.

carelessness, 'erroneous behaviour' (Porte, 1995: 149), 'undisciplined processing' (ibid.: 150) or lapses in concentration as the copier fails to give due attention, perhaps owing to the tedium of the exercise or as a consequence of limited ability. These perspectives have filtered into educational and wider ('Western') societal thinking and have formed mainstream opinion there. For over a century developmental psychologists have been interested in how, under experimental conditions, children copy line, abstract and perspective drawings more or less 'accurately'. Based on the theories of Georges-Henri Luquet (1913) taken up by Jean Piaget with Bärbel Inhelder (1956), earlier research accounted for 'inaccuracies' and 'errors' such as drawing a handle on a cup that cannot be seen as a reliance on 'intellectual realism' as against 'visual realism', or drawing what is known rather than what is seen (Freeman and Janikoun, 1972). This divides thinking and perception. Other explanations for 'incorrect' copies of line drawings of cubes include immature motor skills (Phillips, Hobbs and Pratt, 1978). One argument in adopting this theoretical perspective is that 'inaccuracy' creeps in when children begin to make meaning, for example when an abstract line drawing that looks rather like a table is drawn as a table rather than as an abstract combination of lines (Lee, 1989). From this viewpoint, meaning making is seen to 'interfere' with accurate replication. More recently, it has been contested that so-called 'meaningfulness' (i.e. a drawing that resembles a familiar object) can be beneficial to copying (Sheppard, Ropar and Mitchell, 2005). That children draw what is salient to them (Krascum, Tregenza and Whitehead, 1996) raises questions around whose definition of 'accuracy' counts.

What if Emil's 'mistakes' are looked at again? And what if they are examined in the light of the temporality and embodiment of interpretation and re-production? Even when text making happens in oral silence, a variety of observable features can provide clues to meaning: the order of production (e.g. what the copier does first, looking between source and copy, moving between writing and drawing), choice and handling of media (e.g. swapping from pencil to crayon, applying colour, aligning the graphic surface) and temporal information (e.g. the time taken to produce items, sustained gaze, glancing up, pausing). It is not necessarily that observation of processes of production enables a definitive pinning down of meaning, but that it can provide some insights into certain decisions. Interruptions to flow, for example, can suggest moments of uncertainty or consideration of alternatives.

Emil spoke a number of languages, and was relatively new to English. He looked up at the source text prior to, and once in the midst of, more challenging spellings: 'type', 'liquid', 'amount', 'container', 'measuring', 'of measurement' (Figure 2.2d). A longer gaze than elsewhere, but still one glance only, preceded his writing of 'type'. Adjustment from 'tup' to 'typ' to 'type' 'externalized' the process of reaching a resolution on spelling. One inference is that omission of the letter 'u' in 'measring' and 'measment' is a consequence of carelessness or 'undisciplined processing' (op cit). Alternatively, if, as he read silently, Emil imaginatively 'heard' these words, then his versions would be precise if not conventionally 'correct' transcriptions of the spoken form: in speaking, the 'ur' of 'measuring' can be elided (mɛʒrɪŋ). Emil's teacher commented that his spelling was 'atrocious', that 'he hasn't even spelt evaporation right', and that 'some words in there are very odd'. An alternative to deficiency and inadequacy is interpretation, analysis and remaking.

REDESIGN

In the bounded openness of making a text without direct recourse to another, decisions are reached about which meanings will be made, and how those meanings will be made. Signifying resources are chosen according to their suitability for the particular representational need. If the sign maker selects 'the best, most apt available form for the expression of a particular meaning' (Kress, 1997: 17), then what happens in copying when resources are given? Does copying remove opportunities for selecting apt forms for the expression of meaning? Are principles suspended if features are already given?

Copying is constraining, but there remains scope for redesign. Redesign in copying is concerned with changes that are made in the process of making one text into another. Changes can transform meaning in subtle and significant ways. A modification in one place may provide insights into copied items elsewhere, or it may signify a shift in what the text is. Apparently trifling adjustments such as size, positioning or materiality may not be so trivial after all. In what follows, five kinds of redesign are examined: substitution within and across modal resource 'sets', intensification, and addition in the same and different modes.

Adopting the theoretical approach of sign making rather than sign use, modes of representation and communication provide not signs but semiotic resources. Much is known about the lexis and grammar of writing: its nouns, verbs, adjectives, adverbs, tense, word order, and so on. Taking writing as design, its resources comprise more than language alone. Letters are made in upper or lower case and are presented in some kind of orthographic style or typographic font, and punctuation marks provide resources for framing. Writing can be arranged continuously, in paragraphs, as bullet points, with headings and subheadings, and can be realized with different materialities. Drawing also offers a range of resources: straight and curved lines of different lengths and in numerous configurations, directionality, angle, arrangement, colour, and the application of substance. The countless variations in how these options can be combined provide the potential for endless possibilities for meaning. Co-generated in the act of production, features co-exist in the material product as semiotic ensembles. This co-presence has implications for interpretation, re-production and redesign in copying. Analysis of the design of the source text—its forms and (hypothetical) meanings—and resolutions with regard to what the copy will be presents the 'copier' with an array of options, and a range of decisions. What is recognized, valued and deemed relevant in the variety of ways in which meanings have been made in the original frames what is done in the copy.

When writing is remade as writing or drawing as drawing the source and destination modes are shared. Possibilities for redesign within the mode—or 'intramodal redesign'—are available. The 'copier' may choose to make adjustments within the resource 'set', such as changing tense, substituting one punctuation mark for another, reorienting directionality or reorganizing arrangement. For example, in copying from the board in a science lesson on osmosis (see Chapter 3), Davonte substituted 'My results' for 'My reserloution (resolution)'. The noun begins with the same three letters, but it is a different lexical item with a different meaning. Was this a mistake? It is not identical to the original, but its modification—'my solution to this puzzle'—is entirely apt to the task of suggesting an explanation of what had been observed. It is not at all haphazard, and bears traces of semiotic processes.

Whether or not layout is copied depends on whether it is recognized, and whether it is judged to be significant for the task in hand—or, indeed, whether the 'copier' wishes to adjust or redistribute meaning. Emil retained lexical items—if sometimes with changes to spelling—and he altered positioning. As in his teacher's original, he remade five 'chunks' of written text (Figure 2.2c). The teacher had assembled the features constituting a fair test as a vertically arranged list (Figure 2.2a). Emil's more closely resembles continuous writing (Figure 2.2d). It could be that he did not recognize the significance of arrangement in the succeeding inventory. Actually, what might be judged at first sight to be 'incorrect' turns out to be principled. The size of his writing had implications for what could be done. In abiding by the principle of blocks of text with continuousness of methodological criterion and specification, sustaining the arrangement of this subject matter on one 'line' was not possible. Emil substituted vertical positioning for horizontal spacing. Larger gaps can be seen between some words than others. Their positioning is not at all random; spaces are located between each feature of fair test conditions. The principle of separation is shared, but it is redesigned (and with implications for meaning).

Flexibility in how certain meanings can be made offers opportunities for the intensification of meaning. Graphic emphasis, for example, can be created through relative enlargement, centrality, underlining, framing, animation, colour, line weight, capitalization, font, substance, and so on (Kress and Van Leeuwen, 2006). Hierarchies of salience can be amplified and diminished by adjusting and combining more or less of these signifying resources. A class of 10- and 11-year-olds was learning how to copy and paste from the web using handheld devices. Saafa highlighted the sentence 'There was a "whoosh" and a "bang"'. A hovering stylus over alternative menu options 'externalized' moments of consideration and resolution with regard to modification of graphic appearance. In her redesign, the linguistic signifiers remained identical, but she increased the font size of 'whoosh' and 'bang' and capitalized their initial letters to give increased salience to these key words. Saafa's redesign was not arbitrary.

Adding graphic items beyond those of the original is a form of redesign. This may be within the mode, or 'intramodal'. In this lesson where children were copying and pasting from the web, the task was to 'edit and improve' a narrative so that it 'contains excellent VCOP' (vocabulary, connectives, openers and punctuation). As they moved the stylus sequentially across the writing displayed on the screens of the handheld devices, sometimes simultaneously reading aloud or in an undertone, intonation provided some clues to children's meaning making, but certain meanings were internal, and hence inaccessible. Even so, pausing over words indicated either uncertainty or interest in potential for amendment. The additions children made provide insights into their interpretation of the surrounding copied text and the piece as a whole. In other words, signifiers not shared with the source text can provide glimpses of meanings made of the source text. Altering 'I have just invented a time machine' to 'I have just invented a (an) adventurous amazing time machine' entailed the addition of descriptive vocabulary that hints at the excitement of a forthcoming exploit. It demonstrates that certain features of the text have been read and understood. Discussed during the opening of a literacy lesson in a Reception class, the teacher wrote the date on the board for subsequent copying. Zakariah preceded his with a full version of the year number (Figure 2.4b) and Nabil added 'Fr' for Friday (Figure 2.4c). These

Figure 2.3   'Copying' from a storybook (Nicky).

kinds of divergence are acceptable pedagogically because knowing different ways in which the date can be written is valued educationally.

Where writing is added to a copied image, or drawing to copied writing, redesign becomes multimodal. This enables the 'copier' to construct meaning in interrelationships between the two modal components. Nicky selected three images of spaceships from those available in a storybook. With careful attention to detail, his drawings are remarkably accurate re-productions in terms of outline shape, criterial characteristics and colour (Figure 2.3). Arranged vertically, aligned horizontally and subsequently separated by parallel wavy lines, the spacecraft are presented as key features of this popular phenomenon. This 'conceptual' representation is a shift from the narrative of the storybook source. Nicky excluded background, characters and plot. His addition of the well-known catchphrase names the fiction adventure series and, arguably, capitalization implies its familiar enunciation. At the top of the page, he inscribed the name of the recipient. Why is this apparently trivial addition significant?

RECONTEXTUALIZATION

What is it that guides children's copying? The copier is faced with certain framing issues. How exact does the copy need to be? What is criterial and what can be excluded? Where is there scope for modification or addition? This entails making decisions about the relationship between source and copy in the light of purpose and social context. The 'copier' might decide to copy certain features and not others. Judgements are made about where sameness or similarity should be sustained, and what can be adjusted or supplemented. Children might decide to stay with the same resources as those appearing in the source text, they might choose resources that are similar, or they might select quite different resources. Constancy of wording and punctuation may be retained, whilst font, size and line-by-line matched arrangement of lexical items might be considered irrelevant. These decisions are guided by why the copy is being made and for whom. An instruction to copy may be a means of ensuring that required subject matter is recorded and presented in a suitable way. The features of a fair test elicited from the class were expressed with scientific terminology ('observe', 'evaporated', 'sample', 'measurement') omitting the kind of descriptive vocabulary required in a literacy lesson and with grammatical structures uncomplicated by subordinated clauses, and arranged in a way apt to the representational practices of science (Figure 2.2a). What happens when a source text designed and produced in a different place at a different time is 'copied' for a 'new' purpose? Is subject matter—what the text is about—fixed? Is a copy a replication of the original that can become socially misaligned?

A copy of something is made by someone, for someone, and for a particular purpose. Nicky made his 'copy' one evening as he, members of his family and visitors sat round the dining table (Figure 2.3). Addressing it to a close family friend marks a change of function and a shift in social relations from that of the source. Images in a storybook designed for children became a gift for a godmother. Passionate about this popular craze, and an avid collector of videos, books, plastic figures, toys, games and stickers, this was a way of sharing his enthusiasm with someone he valued (along with the addition of an uncoloured, framed and labelled picture of Tintin—another favourite), just as other people around the table shared their news, plans, views and concerns. This was a redesign with a modified social alignment. What was and was not copied, and what was added, was a response to purpose. The outcome was a graphic artefact, inscribed with the interest of the maker and shaped for the recipient. Meaning making in copying originated in, responded to and reaffirmed the relationship between child and adult.

Copying as re-production and redesign is always contextualized. Social relations, purposes and practices shift. What is done in one environment may or may not be apt to another. The classroom is not only a social space characterized by well-established rules, but also an educational space where certain aspects of knowledge and learning are demonstrated and assessed. Children are schooled into, and quickly learn, the boundaries around what can and cannot be done, how resources are to be used, and the consequences of 'getting it right' or 'getting it wrong'. When instructed to copy,

2.4a Original (reprinted with permission).

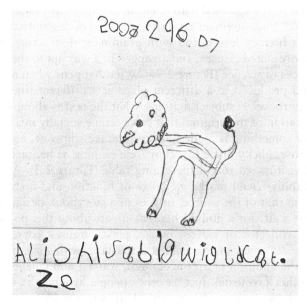

2.4b Zakariah.

they are expected to do so in response to the objectives of the lesson and the practices of the classroom.

Following on from a whole-class phonic activity that entailed articulating sounds in response to illustrated letters, 4- and 5-year-olds in a Reception class searched through picture dictionaries for words beginning with the letter 'l'. Before even beginning the process of producing the 'copy' in

2.4c   Nabil.

2.4d   Miguel.

Figure 2.4   'Copying' from a picture dictionary.

their literacy exercise books, the children made selections. In choosing one extract (Figure 2.4a), three boys eliminated 11 other possibilities, including a large and brightly coloured ladybird at the top left of the left-hand page. They also omitted other salient features of the source text such as the red, wavy-lined square frame enclosing each entry, the red page numbers and the quick reference letter indexes superimposed on a red background. Remaking the text for literacy purposes demanded making selections apt to the task.

A shift in site from a printed publication brought with it rules in how school exercise books can and cannot be used. In each case, continuous written text is re-produced as one block on a horizontal plane. Even so, the children's 'copying' entailed the redesign of layout. The 12 dictionary entities were assembled across a double-page spread in a regularly patterned arrangement. The literacy exercise books consisted of a blank upper area and a lined half underneath. Use of this configuration is tightly regulated in the classroom. In response to habituated practices of writing on lines and drawing in areas of white space, 'copying' the dictionary extract required swapping round the layout of the graphic ensemble. Modification of arrangement was expected, and undertaken, in each case: the writing is positioned below rather than above the image. The boys' 'copies' are alterations shaped towards the rules of the classroom.

Copies have their own material existence. The shift in site constituted not only a spatial relocation, but also marked a shift of identity (here from publisher to student) and purpose (here from reference text to demonstration of learning). Functionality may be shared with the original, such as lists of spellings intended for memorization copied from the class whiteboard into a notebook. In other instances, recontextualization may entail different aims. With the objective of demonstrating their literacy knowledge and skills, re-producing writing from the picture dictionary accurately was an imperative. All of the children wrote before they drew. In each instance, the lettering is identical to that of the extract: 'A lion is a big wild cat.' Whether the boys actually read this was irretrievable, because the writing was not articulated as speech. Even so, each child was meticulous in attending to the form and ordering of letters, with careful attention to shapes that are in a matched sequence. Just one exception is the addition of a 'g' in Zakariah's version of 'wigld (wild)' (Figure 2.4b). If this is a consequence of looking for what followed the letter 'i' somewhere in the middle of the sentence, this may be an incorrect spelling, but it is guided by a principled strategy.

As well as constancies with the original writing, there are changes. Typography became orthography. Zakariah's dots—over the letter 'i' and the full stop—are exaggerated compared with their relative inconspicuousness in the original (Figure 2.4b). Each of the three boys concluded the sentence with the requisite full stop. Descenders (e.g. 'g') may not fall below the line—indeed there is no line in the dictionary extract. In noticing presence rather than absence, the form of letters and punctuation marks seems to have taken precedence over spacing between words. Omission is a sign of agency. In the re-production of copying, something was not re-produced. Exclusion of gaps, something often missing from the writing of beginning writers, provides insights into processes of 'filtering' through children's existing literacy knowledge. Non-recognition of spaces between words, just like the enlargement of dots and adjustments to letter descenders, was an act of interpretation. Framed by the criteria for literacy assessment, absent spacing provides insights into the 'what else' of future learning.

After the 'real' work of the literacy lesson had been completed came the opportunity to draw. Where absolute precision had been required in the re-production of writing, drawing provided greater scope for modification. There are constancies between the boys' drawings of the lion and the source. Each consists of a profile body, a face and an upwardly pointing tail. Excluding background in each 'copy' exacted the addition of paw detail which varies in each instance: Zakariah's hoof-like superimposition, Nabil's continuousness and Miguel's depiction of claws. There are also changes: in outline shape, in the detail of physical attributes, in orientation, in colour and in size. What, actually, is going on here? These young children redesigned an existing design. Processes of redesign are agentive, and there is not necessarily just one solution. The variations in each remaking of the dictionary extract indicate that the boys attended to different aspects of meaning. In the absence of specified criteria for the assessment of drawing in this lesson, it is not that any of the three 'copies' is 'right' or 'wrong', or 'better' or 'worse', but rather that each of the boys redesigned the original image according to his particular interest at that moment in time.

In copying, the lines and shapes of a drawing might be sustained, adjusted slightly or entirely modified. Take the head, for example. Rather than a flowing mane suggested by disconnected black lines of varying weight, length and directionality of the dictionary extract, Zakariah drew a version consisting of connected curly lines at the top, shifting to loops under the muzzle (Figure 2.4b). Diagonal eyebrows and a zigzag mouth are modifications to the dictionary extract (Figure 2.4c). As he drew, Nabil repeatedly intoned to himself and others, 'He's going to eat the fish.' Presumably intended to depict aggression, this addition picks out a distinguishing feature of a lion. The stability of this meaning is retained in the signifiers of the copy, whilst the narrative (that the lion is going to eat the fish) is lost (see Chapter 3). Although not identical, lettering was broadly like the original. With line in drawing, Zakariah and Nabil retained the core meaning of 'maneness' but adjusted its appearance from that of the source. Miguel's attention was directed towards the outline contour of the animal which he re-made precisely as a continuous 'embracing line' (Goodnow, 1977: 45) that includes a curved back, angled hind leg and ears, without specific delineation of the mane (Figure 2.4d). With the educationally less highly valued mode of drawing, greater scope for redesign is legitimized.

These modifications fall within the boundaries of representing 'lionness', but what about more substantial departures? The intramodal redesign of 'copying' offers choice within discrete sets of modal resources (see above). In handmade texts, shading entails a range of options: choice of substance (e.g. wax crayon, pencil crayon, felt tip), colour (from what is available), shade (light or heavy application), coverage (complete or partial) and line (straight in one or multiple directionalities, looped). Each of these offers possibilities for variation. In remaking the dictionary extract, shading became shading, but with shifts in how it was done. Zakariah's even, uniform yellow colouring is closest to the original and would be valued as apt subject knowledge in a science lesson. (Similar, but not identical, to the series of irregular lines of the original, he also added horizontal pencil lines on the body to signify fur.) Nabil distinguished between the fur of the lion's body and its mane by swapping between sky blue and turquoise colouring, the latter more densely applied. Miguel made vertical multi-coloured blocks of blue, red and yellow, with a purple horizontal underside. This might be deemed charming but incorrect. In a lesson where other groups were simultaneously drawing imagined monsters, the provenance of his colouring was contextualized by interest in a concurrent activity.

Is this copying? The texts the boys made are similar, but not identical to the source. They bear likenesses to the original and to one another, but in certain ways they are quite different. If copying is exact replication, are these students failing? An entry in a picture dictionary published for use by young children became a demonstration of learning in the educational framing of a literacy lesson. This demanded recontextualization. Recontextualization in copying entails agentive and principled semiotic work, not random, but shaped by what it that is being done and for whom. In view of the objectives of the activity, decisions are made about which features of the original text must remain constant and where there is scope for omission, change or addition. This entails processes of evaluation. The boys judged what was and what was not legitimate in the pedagogic environment of their classroom. With the objective of demonstrating literacy knowledge and skills, re-producing writing accurately was an imperative. Image provided greater scope for modification. Copying always entails semiotic work. It demands attendance to purpose and social factors. Epistemologically, which features of the source text are selected, and how they are amended and supplemented, provides insights into children's shaping of knowledge. Adjustment from say the second person to the passive voice would mark a shift in social relations. Copied texts are recontextualized in the move across space and time.

DISCUSSION

As with all text making, copying is ideologically framed. What is and is not acceptable shifts. Constancies and changes are more or less suitable and more or less valued depending on purpose. The extent to which copying is condoned, accepted, tolerated, frowned upon, scorned, or condemned is dependent on subject matter, identity, social environment, task and medium: what it is that is being copied, who the copier is, who the copy is for and the rationale for copying. As such, a copy's intellectual, social, aesthetic and moral value varies from context to context. The extent to which the subject matter and social relations constructed in the original are sustained or reshaped in the copy depends on why the copy is being done, and for whom, and this requires purposive social action. Taking account of the framing of purpose, social relations and the representational resources available, investigating copying helps to uncover discourses around contemporary forms of text making.

Even when children are representationally constrained, when their semiotic freedom is restricted, they remain agentive. Re-production in copying is re-presentation where signifiers are shared, and it is for this reason that the meanings the 'copier' has made of the source text may be elusive. Even so, copying entails requisitioning what is needed from the source text in its entirety or in part. Absence of copied features may be a consequence of non-recognition, or may be a deliberate act of remaking that suits the requirements of the 'copier' and the purposes for which the 'copy' is being made. Redesign in 'copying' is concerned with reconfiguration: selections, omissions, substitutions, adjustments, modifications, amendments and additions. Changes are always there, however inconspicuous, and they are always meaningful. They may supplement, extend, deviate from, elaborate or explain that which was given in the original.

Investigating copying requires care. 'Too little credit is given to the work done in copying, yet we can give too much credit too to the 'meaning-making' done through this kind of activity' (Kevin Leander, personal communication). Cause for anxiety around copying in the classroom can be well justified. There are occasions when time could be better spent, such as the laborious copying of learning objectives that children cannot read. A social semiotic approach by no means condones deceit or an avoidance of intellectual effort. On the other hand, selections, retentions and modifications in making a copy can be intensely demanding of initiative. The routine practice of 'copying', commonly considered to be unworthy of attention, turns out to be complex, intriguing and controversial.

3 Ordinariness

Many texts are unremarkable because of their very ordinariness. In the copiousness of their everyday drawing and writing at home and in the routine practices of the classroom, what children do is often apparently unexceptional in terms of audience, subject matter and signifying forms. What if the apparently mundane is looked at through a lens that brings into focus what is generally passed by? Taking seriously, even making strange, the humble recognizes and seeks to understand what occupies children's everyday text making, and how they respond to seemingly run of the mill social, intellectual and representational demands.

MEANING IN THE UNNOTICED

Children's drawing is commonly regarded as a 'natural', innate skill that provides a creative outlet for their aesthetic self-expression. A social semiotic approach shifts the focus to the semiotic work of representation. Made mark by mark, the graphic matter of drawing consists of lines that are straight and curved; one and many; vertical, horizontal and oblique; long and short; thick and thin; close and distant; singly and multiply coloured; fragmented (e.g. dots), continuous (e.g. loops and spirals), adjoined (e.g. zigzags) and connected at each end to make enclosing areas (e.g. circles, squares and triangles). Identical lines and shapes can be selected to make numerous meanings, even within the same drawing. For example, straight lines might represent arms, legs, fingers, eyelashes, the sun's rays, a tree trunk, the ground, a speed line, and so on. What distinguishes them is their length, thickness, number and positioning in relation to one another. These marks are signifiers that 'stand for' something else. Neither replication (Arnheim, 1969), nor a 'print out of the real world' (Olson, 1970: 19), nor 'photographic realism', they are interpretations of objects, places, people, events, ideas, and so on realized materially. Three-dimensionality is shown on a flat surface, size and distance are reconfigured, texture is implied, and relations in time are reshaped as relations in space. Resolutions are reached about what can and cannot be done with the resources available: what to include, omit or modify. The final product is an analytical distillation. At the same time meaning rich and partial, a drawing is not an exact replica of its source materially or experientially. Particularized according to the specification of the task—whether stipulated by someone else or self imposed—and how the text will be evaluated or used, children make decisions about what is needed.

Raising standards in literacy (and numeracy) is an issue that frequently recurs on political agendas and in the press. Educational policy in England over recent years has invested heavily in the development, implementation and monitoring of a literacy 'strategy' (DfES, 2006) which, in relationship with the nationally stipulated curriculum for English (DfEE and QCA, 1999), sets out a detailed framework for learning to read and write in each term of the primary (elementary) phase of schooling. There is no such fully articulated specification of the forms and functions of drawing, or how it should be taught and assessed. Unmentioned in certain programmes of study, notably English (DfEE and QCA, 1999: 42–59), elsewhere, drawing and 'pictures' are by no means ignored, if more predominant at Key Stage One (5- to 7-year-olds) and, in the larger proportion of occurrences, offered as exemplification rather than requirement. Mention of image of any kind is far surpassed by references to 'language' and 'text' (i.e. writing), which are also implied in the frequent occurrences of 'identify', 'describe' and 'explain'. Image is omitted from the 'key skills' to be developed across the curriculum, with communication focusing entirely on speaking, listening, reading and writing (DfEE and QCA, 1999: 20).

In the classroom, being allowed to draw a picture after the 'real' work of writing has been completed sustains the discourse that drawing is an appendage, even a time-filler, that keeps children occupied. One teacher's instruction 'Leaving the picture to the end [...] the important thing is the sentences' makes its subsidiary role absolutely explicit. A more positive view of drawing as a 'way in' for children that alleviates the demands of writing, that provides a means of expression for less confident writers or that motivates engagement because it is perceived as 'fun' sustains the discourse that it is a temporary place holder. The question is whether drawing is a second best substitute for writing, or whether it can offer certain opportunities for children to demonstrate their learning and for teachers to assess that learning. This is by no means to advocate a destabilization of the role of writing, nor to undermine its importance, but rather to make a case for the importance of attending to forms of representation that have relevance in their own place.

Whether or not opportunities for drawing have diminished in primary schooling in England as literacy has taken centre stage, children do draw in the classroom. In learning about the seasons, a Year 2 class (6- and 7-year-olds) completed a worksheet consisting of a doubly outlined circle divided into four quadrants. A tick and the comment 'Super pictures!' (Figure 3.1a) is one instance of the many occasions when teachers look at and respond to children's drawings. Rachel (age 6 years) picked out features of the farming year. Her drawings are clear, neatly outlined and carefully coloured. (Note also her apt choice of the top right as her starting point for sequencing the seasons.) Daniel (age 6 years and the youngest in his year group) received no graphic feedback on his text (Figure 3.1b). At first glance, it might appear less 'mature', with its unclothed 'stick' people, their 90 degree outwardly stretched arms, hands represented as straight lines attached to circles, and unvarying forward-facing directionality. Actually, his text is a highly succinct and accurate representation of the seasons. Daniel represented changing weather: snow (62 circles arranged in vertical lines), sunshine and wind (in the Peircian 'indexicality' (Buchler, 1955: 108–109) of the kite). The recurrence of a tree in each quadrant is not repetition but a series of redesigns. Varying the number, coverage, detail and positioning of leaves is a concise way of capturing the annual cycle of this natural phenomenon. For example, the leaves of autumn are falling, whereas those of winter are fallen; sparseness of leaves in the spring contrasts with dense coverage and fruit in the summer. A hazard of being distracted by features that are suggestive of immaturity is that demonstration of knowledge may be missed.

It is not that this teacher 'failed' to mark adequately. 'Knowing' children through day-to-day contact with them shapes feedback. Whilst being criterion referenced and normative, what qualifies as an acceptable standard is specific to the individual. By commending good effort, marking can be a means of encouragement (Wyatt-Smith and Castleton, 2005: 141). Teachers' assessment of curricular work is contextualized as they factor in their observations and interactions over the course of the lesson (ibid.). Their recollections of what was said and done inform what they recognize as significant in students' demonstration of their learning (ibid.). Even so, it is important that assumptions about 'ability' or maturity do not negatively influence judgements or prevent recognition of the semiotic work in which children engage.

Drawing inanimate objects is one thing. Representing the movements, changing states and events of a dynamic and temporal world on the fixity of the page is another. In drawing, shifts in visual phenomena across space and time are represented as marks on a surface. Decisions must be made about how this will be done. In part, this depends what it is that is being drawn: the changing location of a body from one place to another, a constantly altering visual phenomenon, the unfolding of a sequence of episodic shifts in an event, and so on. The drawing might be an equivalent of a freeze frame, such as the bent limbs and torso of walking, running, bending or catching (Goodnow, 1977: 142–148; Lowenfeld, 1939: 158, 162), or jumping with the person vertically distanced from the ground line (Lowenfeld and Brittain, 1987: 277). Rather like a sequence of photographic shots separated by milliseconds, a series of six action drawings of performing a long jump made by 5- and 6-year-olds show changing body postures, arm and leg shapes and positioning in relation to the ground, as well as footprints and spraying of the sand on landing (Forman, 1998: 176–182). Superimposition of different body positions in representing dance and in preparing to begin a race ('ready, steady, go') can depict movement over time (Sedgwick, 2002: 71–77). A dotted track can indicate a trajectory (Cox, 1992: 66). These ways of drawing people in

3.1a Rachel.

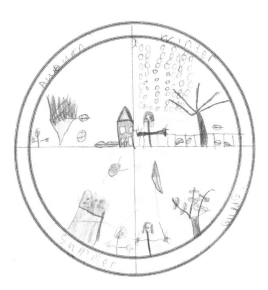

3.1b Daniel.

Figure 3.1 The seasons.

action are generally familiar and acknowledged. Other ways of showing changing form are perhaps less well recognized.

As part of a science topic, the same Year 2 class completed a table classifying sources of light as items powered by mains electricity and batteries, fire and celestial bodies. Katie (age 6 years) chose to draw an aerial firework (Figure 3.2a). Her disconnected pencil lines, numbering over 60 in total, are mainly short and equidistant. Some are longer towards their outermost point. Was this an accident or a consequence of the tedium of repetition? Katie also varied pencil pressure. Heavy application produced bold marks whereas, particularly at the centre bottom of the image, a lighter touch created comparatively paler shades. To judge this as haphazard or slapdash would be a misconstrual of the semiotic work she invested in her drawing. This combination of intensity and length seems to represent the motion of an explosion, when multiple single sparks shoot outwards with different intensities of light, strong at the epicentre and fading as the sparks travel and dissipate. Katie partially coloured her image in bold bands of red, pale blue and brown and purple. As in a previous drawing of a firework, the directionality of her colouring strokes, straight rather than looped or multidirectional, follows an unswerving outward trajectory. This appears to represent the firework's outburst of colour, the intensity of her shading presumably representing its brightness. Katie's drawing invites the imagined recall of changing visualities.

In drawing her firework in response to the same task, Rachel (whose 'seasons' text was examined above) made a variety of meanings in her choice and combination of resources (Figure 3.2b). Shades are blended in her superimposition of repeated multicoloured strokes to represent an indeterminate spectrum of hues in an eruption of colour. Gentle application creates semi-transparency rather than opacity, as apt to the ephemerality of a firework. The slightly curved, upward trajectory of her crayon strokes imitates the rising motion of a fountain-like firework. Temporality and movement are everywhere implied through the varying lengths and uneven endpoints of her lines which suggest the different rates at which the flying sparks fade.

If semiotic features are not recognized they cannot be assessed. Some signifiers of drawing are more immediately noticed than others, some are barely acknowledged and others are overlooked. Pencil pressure (heavy or light application to create shades), extent of shading (partiality or complete coverage), directionality of stroke (e.g. monodirectional or multidirectional), range of colour (separation and superimposition) and line endpoints (flush and uneven) are resources children select and combine in their making of meaning. Drawing tends to be subject to some caution, if not suspicion, and is generally not invested with the same level of confidence as writing (or speech). Concerns about reading too much into children's drawings are not so far removed from anxieties as to whether they are valid and reliable—or at least as valid and reliable as what is said or written. Perhaps

3.2*a*　Katie.

3.2*b*　Rachel.

Figure 3.2　Fireworks.

this should be counterbalanced by taking seriously the intricacy of their drawing. Recognizing children's semiotic efforts invests trust in the sincerity of their representation. Even within the mode of drawing (and of writing), certain features are attended to in preference to, even to the exclusion of, others. If children make meaning in a variety of ways, then all aspects of their designs warrant acknowledgement. Holding back from overly hasty dismissal of less well-recognized features and opening out to the possibility of meaning in unforeseen places takes seriously the semiotic plenitude of their texts.

MEANING IN MAKING

Simultaneous actions, gestures, talk and vocalization as children draw can provide insights into how they connect form and meaning, and the volatility of sign making. In the absence of the recipient of the text in the process of making and denied an opportunity for supplementary explanation, drawing (and writing) must be sufficient of itself to convey certain meanings. This requires that ambiguity be restrained. The meanings associated with certain signifiers are sufficiently stable to be suited or unsuited to particular signifieds, such as a peer's drawing of a racing car described as 'vroooom' being deemed inappropriate for a 'nice car' (Holm Hopperstadt, 2008a: 90). In interpreting the meanings suggested by certain material features, children explore their semiotic potentialities. Signifying forms may not necessarily have one meaning only, as children 'play' with their own mark making and that of others (Cox, 2005: 121; Holm Hopperstadt, 2008a). Alternative meanings for the same signifier may be posited on the basis of the suggestiveness of form: hair was interpreted as a hat and an angel as a butterfly (Holm Hopperstadt, 2008a: 83). Even as they are produced materially, meanings connected with certain signifiers are not necessarily fixed, and can shift from moment to moment and from person to person. One meaning can give way to another: a rainbow became a sneeze and a zebra became rain (Cox, 2005: 119). What was one thing can become something else and sometimes yet something else again as the drawer's interest shifts in response to the suggestiveness of form (Pahl, 1999: 17–31). This is, in part, why asking children to talk about their drawings after completion produces different kinds of data: it is an interpretation of what was done. The meanings associated with signifying forms are bounded, but not necessarily fixed. For this reason, texts may or may not retain definitive meaning beyond the framing of the episode, and hypothetical recovery of meaning may be inconclusive. A social semiotic approach may not set out to definitively pin down meaning, but rather to investigate meaningfulness.

There is a dynamic relationship between interpretation, design and production. Developmental psychologists devised an experiment to investigate how 3- to 6-year-olds' drawings of the human figure follow the axis created by the positioning of the eyes (Goodnow and Friedman, 1972). What is fascinating from a social semiotic perspective is how the children interpreted what was given and designed an apt response. Presented with a circle containing two dots positioned horizontally in the lower quarter of its circumference and asked to make this into a person, resolutions included squeezing in facial features below and drawing figures upside down on a trapeze or standing on their heads (Goodnow, 1977: 75; Goodnow and Friedman, 1972: 13). So what would happen if the two dots were positioned vertically just inside the circle's left arc (Goodnow and Friedman, 1972: 14)? Children responded by representing recumbence—a person lying in bed and 'in the pool looking up'—or making the given representation into a clown, an alien or an animal (Goodnow, 1977: 76–77). They made meaning of what was given and shaped their designs in response to the specified task.

Texts are pre-planned to a greater or lesser extent, and ongoing design decisions continue in the temporal process of production. Made mark by mark, the act of drawing and writing is time-based and therefore sequential. Even as it is being produced, the emerging material text is a semiotic entity with which the maker engages. To a greater or lesser extent, the process of drawing and writing is one of adjustment. What has already been inscribed establishes the ground for subsequent decisions; it can inform, be suggestive of or even demand modification of what comes next. The maker engages with the emerging text and evaluates its sufficiency—how well suited it is to the representational need—and proceeds accordingly. Decisions about which meanings to make and which semiotic resources are apt, how, why, where and when are prior to and ongoing throughout material production.

The semiotic plenitude of drawing as a representational event—the text in its broader sense—does not necessarily inhere in the graphic product alone. The lines, shapes and intense shading of 5-year-old Ben's maps had very particular meanings in the context of his small world enacted and narrated fantasy dramas (Barrs, 1988). Although early studies sometimes logged the sequence of drawing (Goodnow, 1977: 63), they did not report on related interactional exchange, and even considered talk to be 'romancing' (Gardner, 1980: 46)—an oral compensation for a purported deficit in visual 'equivalence'. As children draw, their simultaneous talk names, plans, comments on, describes, narrates, discusses, explains, questions and evaluates (Barrs, 1988; Buckham, 1994; Coates, 2002; Cox, 2005; Holm Hopperstadt, 2008b). This is not merely compensatory, but is rather a dynamic interplay between making meaning on the page and related interaction both with others and externally with themselves.

As what is drawn or written is observed by or shared with co-present others such as the dynamism of dyadic exchange between parent and toddler (Lancaster, 2001), or becomes semi-public in grouping around tables in the classroom, material actualization enables those others to engage with the emerging text. Multimodal, interactions around drawing and writing can consist of combinations of spoken exchange (e.g. remarks, questions, advice, suggestions and criticisms), articulation (e.g. laughing, sniffing), gaze (e.g. glancing, sustained watching), facial expression (e.g. smiling, grimacing) and gestures (e.g. pointing, nodding). This can influence what is done. What is recorded and how is shaped by topics that are introduced, explored, negotiated, ignored and taken up. Shaped by the evaluation of others as they show interest, approbation, disagreement or puzzlement in response to the unfolding of an emerging text, the text maker may disregard, take note of, compromise or engage with feedback, and decline or assent to it. Grounded in the immediacy of what is going on and who is involved, interactions with others during the process of production distributes what is represented and how. Although made materially by one individual, texts can be multiply sourced, and hence have sometimes traceable and sometimes indeterminate semiotic provenance (see Chapter 6).

Through bodily sign making, children sometimes enact motion that has meaning tied to the phenomenon that they are representing graphically. In 'gestural' or 'actional' representation, they mimic movements and events they have observed in their everyday experience, such as dots for running or jumping feet hitting the ground (Vygotsky, 1978: 107) or a rabbit hopping (Wolf and Perry, 1988: 20). Dramatizing zigzags, arcs, ellipses and dots was a response to the immediacy of simultaneous thunder, lightening and heavy rain (Matthews, 1999: 1–3). Repeated circles captured the movement of a big wheel, overlaid loops depicted bubbles rising to the surface and staccato stabbings signified a sneeze (Matthews, 1998: 93–95).

A class of 8- and 9-year-olds was learning about osmosis; a flower had been placed in a cup of water mixed with red food dye one week previously. Scientific inquiry in the primary classroom in England requires that students 'try to explain how living things and non-living things work, and to establish links between causes and effects' through 'systematic observations' (DfEE and QCA, 1999: 83). As groups discussed why plants need a stem, the teacher picked up on an earlier comment Nathan had made about the flower collecting water, and twice probed further regarding its movement (Table 3.1a–c, f–h). In the dynamism of the exchange, it might appear that Nathan 'just parroted' Moiz who, on both occasions, supplied the answers (Table 3.1b–c, i–j). Actually, Nathan participated in and contributed to the group's co-construction of knowledge, and demonstrated his own his learning, through gesture in relation to his drawing. He stroked his image of the stem slowly from base to flower head, then down and back again more rapidly, with matched and synchronized rocking of his upper body (Table 3.1d). Subsequently, as his teacher asked, 'So what travels through what?' Nathan did not only repeat the reply made by Moiz (Table 3.1j–k) but also traced his finger up and down his representation of the stem a further 13 times (Table 3.1k–l). In the distribution of collaborative learning, Nathan enacted the movement of osmosis through gestural interaction with his drawing.

The lesson objective was to 'make careful observations and present those observations using drawing' and to suggest a scientific explanation for redness in the petals. Given increased significance by the teacher's intervention, or maybe because it had enabled Nathan to learn something he had not known previously, following on from this exchange he went on to rule a red horizontal line about a quarter of the way up from the base of his stem and to superimpose his green shading with red (Figure 3.3a). This represents the part that had been dipped in food dye, as Kai later pointed out, 'It was like green there but then all down there was red.' Nathan also added an inner band running along length of the remainder of the stem and overlapping the lowermost petal. Why did he do this? This is not what he could see. Children sometimes include in their drawings what is actually occluded, such as the contents of a gorilla's stomach to show what it ate for dinner (Cox, 1992: 122). The brownish hue shows the internal: the food dye inside the green stem, what is within the 'tube'. In a subsequent interview, Nathan explained:

'What I did (..) 'cos I done this bit of food colouring here (.) and then it went up to the petal (..) then there was all little lines of red on.'

His theorization is not restricted to writing. Drawing provided a means of showing the process of osmosis.

Table 3.1 Interactions around Drawing (19 seconds)

	Teacher		Nathan		Moiz	
	Speech	Gesture	Gesture	Speech	Gaze	Speech
a)	does it just collect the water?				teacher	
b)					Moiz	no
c)	or does it travel through it?				teacher	it travels up the tube
d)			strokes his drawing of the stem slowly from base to flower head, down and back again more rapidly, with synchronous rocking of his upper body		drawing, quick glance at Moiz	
e)				and into the	drawing	
f)	it travels through it	places her finger at the base of Nathan's drawing of the stem	keeps his index finger placed at the con-junction of the stem and the petal	tube (barely audible)	teacher	
g)	so what travels				drawing	
h)	through what?				teacher	
i)					teacher	water
j)			raises, lowers and raises again his right palm	water	teacher, Moiz	tube
k)			touches the bottom of his drawing of the stem in the same place as his teacher had previously, and moves his finger up and down the stem seven times	tube	drawing, teacher	
l)			continues to move his finger up and down a further six times		drawing	

Assessment criteria set out in school curricula in England privilege certain modes of representation above others. This frames what teachers are 'allowed' (Foucault, 1981) to see. Enactment (if recognized at all) is less valued than speech, and image is generally considered to be an inferior mode of representation in contrast with the high value placed on writing. 'Pictures' and 'drawings', along with 'simple' diagrams, appear in the earlier 'levels' of the 'attainment targets' of using and applying mathematics, scientific enquiry, and design and technology (DfEE and QCA, 1999). The view that drawing is merely an illustrative embellishment that accompanies the 'real' work of writing has persisted in education, with the consequence that children receive little formative feedback on what they have drawn in contrast with frequent judgements about achievements in and targets for their written work (Anning, 1999: 169; Christensen and James, 2000: 168; Kenner, 2000a: 69; Millard and Marsh, 2001: 55). Whilst judgements about educational acceptability are made and are made accurately with regard to nationally specified levels of subject attainment, there is a danger that the detail of children's drawing remains largely unnoticed and that features of learning might be missed because drawing is not a mode of representation featuring in contemporary forms of assessment.

In response to the reports on osmosis, the teacher's marking did not disregard the diagrams but focused more particularly on writing. Apart from two comments that pointed out what were judged to be errors (colouring the whole flower red and the inclusion of roots), responses to drawings consisted of either ticks (check marks) and / or 'well done' (occurring 15 times), with no feedback at all in three instances. The teacher explained that this was necessary in view of regimes of testing in force at that time. She made an average of four responses to writing on each of the 20 texts. The 22 ticks signifying approbation were particularized as praise such as 'Well done—great observations'. Non-scientific terminology was pointed out and sometimes an alternative was offered (e.g. underlining of 'sucked' and suggestion of 'transport'). Writing took precedence over drawing.

Teachers' marking of curricular work is generally one-way; it is fixed and final. Occurring 17 times, the most common question was 'What job does the stem do?' In just one isolated instance, Semmy subsequently responded in writing: 'It ~~sucks~~ transports the water from the stem to the petals' (Figure 3.3b). The deletion of 'sucks' and its replacement with a more scientific term is a connection with the teacher's instruction to 'use the word transport' inscribed above. Dialogic exchange on the page offers one way of sustaining and extending engagement and learning, but this would entail additional workloads for already overloaded teachers. In a packed day and with a heavy curriculum, there is little time for returning, reviewing and re-engaging. Even so, contained time to read graphic feedback and managed opportunities for revisiting and debate could support children's learning.

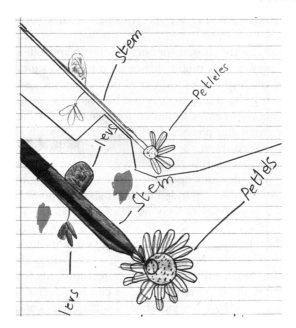

3.4a   Nathan.

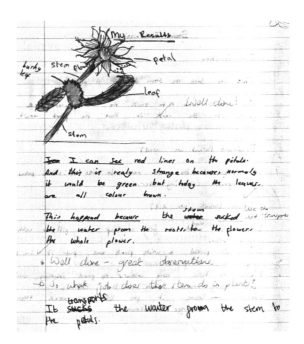

3.4b   Semmy.

Figure 3.3   Osmosis.

MAKING MEANING WITH WHAT HAS BEEN DISCARDED

Signifying resources are chosen for their semiotic aptitude (Kress, 1997). In imaginative play, a stick might suffice for a horse (Vygotsky, 1978: 97), but it has to be the 'right' stick. Material properties such as length, thickness, weight and strength may or may not be deemed criterial in signifying a horse-for-riding that can be mounted for enacting trotting, cantering or bucking. If the particular physical features of a horse such as coat, ears or tail, are also required, then the smoothness of the bark, colour, and the presence or absence of protuberances may be attributes that must be semiotically apt. Aptness depends upon the particular meaning to be made and directs which features are attended to. This shapes choice. A stick suited to representing a horse may or may not do for a wand or a flute, but it is unlikely to be chosen as a teacup or a blanket. There may be a suspension of the fact of 'treeness' in favour of imagined 'horseness'—that which Vygotsky (1978: 97) calls 'severing' meaning—but there is also an inventive process of seeking out, identifying and selecting signifying features. Objects are requisitioned with an eye to meaning as children decide on the relevant attributes of that which is to be signified. Their choices entail processes of analysis with regard to the physical characteristics of items, and imagination with regard to their semiotic possibilities. Selections are not random, but principled. They are made according to the aptness of their signifying potentialities pertaining to their possibilities for meaning.

Just as children choose from whichever sticks are available to signify a horse-for-riding, in their drawing and writing they select media resources from those available to them according to the particular meanings they wish to make. Material properties can be more or less suggestive of possibilities for meaning. Paper comes in different weights, qualities and quantities, and its availability depends on institutional and socioeconomic variables. A blank sheet holds the potential for ready adjustment by turning it into a landscape or portrait alignment. As a bounded area framed by its own edges, it might be suited to purpose as it is, and it also has potential for extension and alteration. Children act upon the surfaces they have chosen because they will not always do as they are: they cut, tear, fold, crumple, wrap, bend, open, take apart, staple, stick together, colour over, etc. Making the most of these opportunities for modification, they construct meaning with size, shape and concealment as they create booklets, greetings cards, pop-ups and envelopes. These kinds of alterations demonstrate children's recognition of the material properties and semiotic potentialities of surface subject to reshaping in some way.

Writing and drawing cannot exist apart from their materiality; graphic marks are made with something on something. Semiotic decisions with regard to the materiality of representation are made as part of the process of design. On the page, drawing and writing entail the application of some sort of substance with an inscriptional instrument. As with surface, different substances have particular potentialities and constraints, and this, in part, constructs possibilities for meaning. Green glitter pen was a choice well suited to the sparkle of Shakira's glittering heroes (Figure 1.1). Drawing a self-portrait with a pencil sharpened to a point was apt to showing the detail of teeth and eyelashes, whereas the broad marking surfaces of pastels allowed Gareth to shade large areas with ease, and to smudge assorted hues with his fingers to blend and modulate variations in skin and hair colour. Felt-tip pens, often a favourite at home, produce bold and fluorescent colours and enable intense coverage. Semiotic decisions with regard to the materiality of representation are unavoidable, whether made by the text maker or someone else.

Kerry (age 7 years) tore along the perforations of tractor-feed paper to detach a single sheet, and selected the plain, cream side as the front rather than the reverse which was printed with pale green stripes. A critical design decision was to remake the graphic frame. Just detectable at various points around the periphery of the heart shape is a pencil outline, which Kerry subsequently cut round with care (Figure 3.4). Why did she do this? Why did she consider a heart drawn, decorated and annotated on a sheet of paper to be inadequate to her semiotic needs? In removing the extraneous space surrounding her outline, Kerry created something that was not a picture on a page. It became an item with its own framing. Children do draw and cut out representations in order to make objects for use: badges to display their interests or successes, crowns, helmets and other headgear that can be worn to establish identity in role play, and figures and objects for small world narrative play. Kerry's heart is not an object for use as such, but she went on to make it into an artefact that can be handled and manipulated.

Children recognize semiotic potentials in what has been discarded. An arrow cut from brown cardboard is threaded through two parallel slits strengthened with sticky tape. Ripping and creasing are evidence of the challenge of accomplishing this feature of her design. Placed rather than permanently affixed, the arrow has some movement. The thick, tough, internally corrugated, difficult-to-cut card provides sturdiness to the fragile and easily torn paper. Kerry could have made her arrow from the same material as her heart. Flimsier even than standard photocopying paper, this would have been much easier to deal with, but it would not have given the final product the same rigidity. The finished 'thing' is not only a design that can be displayed and looked at. Unlike a representation on a sheet of paper, its potential for movement makes it something that can be acted upon.

Kerry communicated meaning with surface as well as on it. The artefact (a heart shape pierced with an arrow as a conventional metaphor for love) and her representations on it (energetic purple rays and green zigzags, the writing 'I love you' and the repeated letter 'x' to represent kisses) are a cohesive orchestration of meaning. In a mutual amplification of the affective, Kerry co-constructed meaning through the crafting of surface and the

Figure 3.4   Heart message (Kerry).

shaping of representation on it, the one intensifying the other. These are deliberately coordinated design decisions.

DISCUSSION

The richness of children's text making is remarkable in its very ordinariness. Neither haphazard nor accidental, in their routine drawing and writing, children shape meaning through their (bounded) choice and combination of a whole range of semiotic resources according to what and whom the text is for. The commonplace is replete with initiative, inventiveness, imagination and ingenuity. This has implications for recognition. To disregard the range of features in children's texts—the ways in which they combine and interrelate resources and meanings—is to overlook aspects of the semi-otic work in which they engage and the semiotic plenitude of their texts.

Interpretation of children's texts demands semiotic work of the inter-preter, and this is not always straightforward. There is not necessarily a neat route in tracing meaning and, in any case, meanings are not neces-sarily definitive. What was meant may be no longer accessible, and what was done may be subject to alternative explanations. Communicational exchange in face-to-face interaction may not be lost in terms of what chil-dren recollect and learn, but it may or may not be represented in their drawing and writing. What is drawn or written is always a selection. Being present during the act of production can provide insights into the meanings children make in their texts. Even so, it is not possible to track every nuance of children's meaning making. The semiotic work of evaluation and assess-ment demands a flexible, open and reflexive semiotic disposition in recog-nizing meaningfulness, and that meanings can shift. As children represent their knowledge, experience and feelings, acknowledging, if not necessarily understanding, the semiotic effort they invest in their text making shows respect for what they do. The signs made in drawing and writing might be puzzling and interpreting their meanings might be hypothetical, but they are traces of the semiotic work in which children have engaged.

4 'Getting it Wrong'

A social semiotic perspective contests that all text making is principled. Even so, children do not always 'get it right' in their writing and drawing. This raises theoretical and practical questions around how text making might be understood as at the same time principled and 'incorrect'. Amendment of children's own texts and response to the advice of others are judgements regarding suitability in the evaluation of aptness in relation to purpose. What are the implications for 'getting it wrong' in and beyond the classroom? How are 'errors' handled in different social environments?

AMENDING WHAT IS 'WRONG'

Design entails consideration of alternative possibilities. In making certain selections, other options are rejected. These processes might be more or less visible as design challenges and resolutions are 'externalized' in the act of production. Hesitation in the flow of production observable in gaze (e.g. examining a graphic feature, looking away), articulation (e.g. sighing, sniffing, clearing the throat, humming), actions (e.g. tapping, head shaking), facial expression (e.g. smiling, frowning) and bodily posture (e.g. slumped, concealing) can be embodied signs of uncertainty, delight and decision making—although making unfounded assumptions can be hazardous. Moments of problem solving, sometimes occurring over fractions of a second, can be observed. For example, Rashida (age 9 years) simulated inscriptional possibilities by tracing with her finger prior to committing herself to the addition of bars in her partly constructed graph. The deliberation with which children select and produce certain signifier resources in preference to others may be more or less pronounced, but choices are always made from a wider or narrower range of possible alternatives. Judgements are made about what can and cannot be done, and what will and will not be done. Something is preferred, or required, on this occasion, over something else.

Graphic texts sometimes bear traces of changes in design decisions. In handmade representations, adjustment, overwriting and crossing out, and the marks and indentations left by erasing are signs of choices that subsequently proved unsuitable and were removed or replaced. For example, Megan erased two circles (presumably representing heads) and repositioned them (see Figure 7.2a). In producing her transcript, Ella (age 11 years) was committed to giving as full and precise an account of the interview as possible (see Chapter 7). There are only rare alterations in her writing. Just 19 (generally zigzag) deletions and four overlays from a total of 1,205 words—just under 2%—are traces of what she deemed to be errors. A number of these are perceived slips in spelling (e.g. 'efect̶affect', 'differen̶dt'). Other amendments suggest revisions made as part of the complex process of transcription. Ella's careful attention to the identity of the speaker and meticulous attention to detail are apparent when she reallocated 'but he wasn't' to the other participant and removed the words 'Hey hey', presumably considering them inaccurate. Her corrections are one trace of her seriousness in the production of an accurate transcript. Aptness is weighed up and features are retained or modified. Each mark and removal of mark represents the semiotic settling of the text maker on fitness for purpose at this moment in time.

Traces of problem solving may or may not be evident in the final product. Some inscriptions can be removed without trace, such as smoothing sand and wiping marks in condensation. Using non-permanent pen on a shiny surface, Hollie wiped away 'geth' and 'er' in an above / below positioning, with her finger and replaced this with continuous, if squashed, lettering (see Figure 6.1d). This was lost in the final product. On the computer, amendments and modifications can be made retrospectively and without trace (e.g. deletion, substitution), graphic items can be subsequently altered through adjustment of font, size, positioning, image effects (e.g. blurring) and so on, and images and writing can be assembled and rearranged with ease. This enables design to be separated out into different phases of production. What is inscribed and erased does not necessarily represent every possibility that was considered and discarded. Absence of amendments may camouflage the internal drama of challenge and compromise of which there may be no graphic trace. The signs made in the material product are those things ultimately deemed apt for the particular representational purpose.

Even from the youngest age, drawn and written texts are predominantly created by one individual. During observations in nursery (kindergarten) settings, writing or drawing on someone else's page was an occasion for indignation and complaint. Collaborative text making is relatively uncommon in the classroom, and also in the home. As child animators worked together in co-design and co-production, accord and disparity were 'externalized' in multimodally constituted debate, negotiation and resolution (see Chapter 7). Three girls took on and swapped roles as they pooled their expertise. Interactions over the course of making the stop-frame animation provide insights into their joint shaping of meaning. For significant periods of time, the children spoke mainly single words. Taken alone, frequent repetitions of 'action' (to signal that the shot could be taken) and 'shoot' (to alert the moment of clicking the shot) in the audio transcript alone might suggest that the activity was merely procedural, even dull. Actually, speech was frequently absent as the embodied communication of action, gesture and gaze carried the semiotic load of the girls' interactions. Harmonized movement and manipulation of the small world figures over stretches of time were periods of smoothness when the children shared design intentions and worked in concert towards agreed goals. It was in moments of uncertainty seen in a hovering hand or hesitating fingers, and conflict of interest as struggles with the figures, nudging away, disapproving gaze and spoken contention that problem solving and decision making with regard to resource and meaning became explicit. A disagreement between Ebony and Ambareen over the orientation of a plastic figure as the children engaged seriously in jointly designing the animation embodied alternative viewpoints (see also Goodwin, 2000). Their difference of opinion over the orientation of the figures and their resolution was multimodally constituted in the girls' actions, gaze and speech (Table 4.1), with talk not always carrying the greater proportion of the semiotic load (see also Flewitt, 2005). This was significant for the development of the plot. Ebony brought to bear the power of the teacher's advice in upholding her view. Jeselle, whilst not entering into the dispute, brought the argument to a close in her role as technician, as the camera had been moved in the course of the altercation. Although Ebony's preference prevailed, Ambareen had the last word. In collaborative activities such as this, alternative possibilities for design and their resolutions can be observed.

WHEN 'GETTING IT WRONG' IS ACTUALLY 'GETTING IT RIGHT'

Text making is social action. It is socially derived, socially framed, socially shaped and socially regulated, and it is also socially responsive, socially negotiated and socially contested. This does not apply only to adults. Children, too, are social agents. They invest serious semiotic effort as they engage with others.

> 'Children are and must be seen as active in the construction and determination of their own social lives, and the lives of those around them and the societies in which they live. Children are not just passive subjects of social structures and processes' (Prout and James, 1997: 8).

Children are shapers of social relationships through their writing and drawing. As active text makers, they engage in, notice and interpret practices, and also sustain, resist, negotiate and transform them (Gee, 2000: 190).

In a child-only online club, the medium of the computer was significant inasmuch as the design of the environment provided certain communicational

Table 4.1 Collaborative Design (plain = Ebony; italics = Amareen; bold italics = Jeselle.

Action	Gaze	Speech	Time
lowers both hands towards her figure, hesitates, and then turns it 90 degrees *grasps her figure but does not move it*	own figure	***action!***	2 seconds
raises then lowers left hand towards her own figure			
grasps Ambareen's figure and turns it *points in the opposite direction*	Ambareen's figure	turn it away	1 second
moves her figure forwards slightly *turns her figure back*	own figure	*no! this's going this way!*	2 seconds
grasps Ambareen's figure and turns it back again *resists*	Ambareen's figure	no!	3 seconds
struggle between the girls	*Ebony*	*he's going there!*	
	Ambareen's figure	no! that one's going this way!	
pushes her figure towards Ebony's *retains her grasp on Ambareen's figure*	*Ebony* own figure Ambareen's figure	*Ebony!* *this one's going to go there!*	1 second
points towards Ebony's figure, *knocks the camera* *retains her grasp on Ambareen's figure, moves her own figure*	Ambareen's figure	*that one's going to go there!*	4 seconds
struggle continues	Ambareen *Ebony to Ebony's figure*	Miss said to do it that way	
continues to grasp her figure lets go and then re-grasps	own figure screen	***you're moving the camera and I can only see one now***	2 seconds
places the figures close together and back to back *Ambareen withdraws*	screen	move it back	3 seconds

Continued

Table 4.1 Continued

accidentally knocks over her own figure	screen	then we've got to walk off	1 second
lifts and repositions her figure	own figure *Ebony's figure*		1 second
	screen	*shoot!*	2 seconds

opportunities. Digital notes—or 'stickies'—were a popular resource. Similar to what are known in England as 'post-its' in shape and representational size, the sticky messages were short. Their limited graphic space (a maximum of around 44 characters) presupposed brevity. Of the 28 posted to Nicola (see Chapter 2) and appearing at the bottom of her home page, the shortest comprised two words ('nice site' and 'Hi nics!'). Longer messages continued on the virtual 'back', but they were never extensive. The content of these e-notes was economical and pithy. Email messaging would have provided scope for more expansive detail, but the children rarely chose this, almost exclusively preferring stickies. Brevity is not necessarily a sign of inadequacy. Here, concision was apt to the communicational practices of the environment. Shortness was also a consequence of haste and the desire for immediacy; these messages were sent and received excitedly, often in the limited time available in a lunchtime club. Irrespective of length, the children invested semiotic work in their design of these messages.

Stickies were used in a way not unlike instant messaging. Nicola and her school friends chatted (e.g. 'Hi Nic i just seen your bro!'), gossiped (e.g. 'I think it was Ben or connor! tried to phone'), 'whispered' intelligences (e.g. 'Pippa crowson is online!') and made plans (e.g. 'If I am not allowed to sleep at your house...'). Used synchronously, children marked their entering and leaving (e.g. 'I'm going now see U sone (soon)' and 'I'm back online now!'). Another main function of sticky exchange was to make contact with club members they did not know and were unlikely to meet face-to-face (e.g. 'hi! my names sophie!'). A common feature of sticky content was response to web page design (e.g. 'Oh Ma GoD Ur PaGeS R WICkEd'). Novel, attractive and impressive materials were commented on and change was monitored (e.g. 'Bril new stuff'). Related to this, club members both sought and shared highly valued technical know-how (e.g. 'Hi! Could you tell me how 2 do that').

'Painstakingly produced' (Burnett et al., 2006: 17), it is immediately apparent that this is not the kind of writing that would be apt in the classroom (see also Carrington, 2004; Merchant, 2005). Was this inadequacy, a failed attempt at 'proper' writing? Alternatively, was it a dismissal of the rules of school-like writing in this out-of-school context? If so, why had children considered it apt to ignore what they had been taught to be 'correct' English usage? The children's lexical choices and grammatical constructions in sticky writing (and chat) were shaped by and for the informality of this child-only environment: abbreviations (e.g. 'bro' rather than 'brother'), conversational forms (e.g. 'soz' in favour of 'sorry') and pet names (e.g. 'nic' and 'nics' as familiar versions of 'Nicola') were highly apt to the kind of language used in socializing with peers. A speech-like register was also apparent in greetings such as 'hay' and 'hi', as well as frequent elisions (e.g. 'I'm') and clipping (e.g. 'comin' rather than 'coming'). Wording such as 'U comin' in preference to 'Are you coming?' and 'I just seen' rather than 'I have just seen' or 'I've just seen' also marks a disjunction between the syntactical constructions of sticky messaging and the curricular writing of the classroom.

Contemporary formal writing is characterized by standardized spelling. Conformity is in part a matter of convenience in that it enables the ready sharing of meaning. It is also subject to educational, political and 'high culture' control which strives to maintain its 'purity' (Halliday, 1989: 30). Spelling is a key feature of teaching and assessment in primary literacy (DfES, 2006). It is when there is disparity from the formal writing of the curriculum—as in the sticky messages—that the ordinariness of everyday spelling in the classroom can be re-seen as the social and cultural phenomenon that it is. As they participated in the practices of the online environment, the children recognized, sustained and invented spellings unlike those of formal writing. Texting-like, they omitted vowels in a kind of shorthand, as in written Hebrew, and made letter swaps (e.g. 'plz' rather than 'please'). Words were abbreviated (e.g. 'pic' in preference to 'picture'). Letter names and numbers represented words (e.g. 'r u' not 'are you' and '2' instead of 'to') (see also Bissex, 1980). As in wider informal practices, the messagers' spelling was neither a fully developed nor an entirely regularized system—just as historically, there was no aim for uniformity of spelling in Medieval England (Clanchy, 1993: 128). It required either knowledge of established texting practices or sufficient security with 'traditional' spelling to imagine new possibilities. Message makers had to appreciate the variant meaning potentiality of letters and numbers, and message receivers had to be flexible in interpreting them for different functions and in different combinations. A primary concern in designing messages is being understood. Whilst choosing familiar texting-like spellings or creating their own, the sticky messagers retained formal spellings for criterial content words such as 'visit' ('Visit mine plz'), 'lessons' ('av 2 go 2 lessons now') and 'game' ('I have just played ur game!').

From the first year of formal schooling in English schools, most 5- and 6-year-olds are expected to use capital letters and full stops in 'simple sentences' (DfES, 2006: 25) and, by the end of Key Stage One (age 7 years), to use 'upper and lower case letters appropriately within words' (ibid.: 27).

There are high stakes in getting this right. Children's use of punctuation marks and letter case in school is unremarkable in its ordinariness, but it is by no means meaningless. It demonstrates their knowledge that this particular deployment of semiotic resources is expected in formal genres. Children recognized differences between sticky notes and writing for curricular purposes, commenting that it released them from the demands of learning the complex rules of punctuation, as in this interview contribution from Leah (age 10 years):

> 'When you're in class you have to make your arm ache to write things for the teacher that are never actually going to see the light of day (.) so it's not really going to be much worth except for learning things (..) but with computers you learn to type (.) how to type in with double hands (.) and also you don't have to always put in punctuation because it's sending to kids [...] they're not really going to care (.) they're just going to want to know what's going on I think [...] I don't like it when the teacher bosses you about and says 'No that's not right' and stuff (.) and 'Oh you haven't put your capital letter in there' (.) or it's just a one off (.) or 'You haven't put a full stop here' (.) and 'Oh no it's all wrong it's all wrong you'll have to write it out all over again' (..) and I'm thinking 'Oh this is boring uuuh!' (..) and then when you're on the net you don't get funny squiggly lines or the teacher shouting in your ear hole.'

What was distinctive about the sticky notes and synchronous chat in this online environment was how they were, and were not, punctuated. School rules were regularly abandoned. Texting-like, capitalization was notable by its absence in places where it would normally be expected in curricular work; it was often omitted at the beginning of texts where it would be obligatory in formal writing and it was not always used for names (e.g. 'hi! my names sophie!' would look very different as 'Hi! My name's Sophie!'). This might be partly to do with the speed of composition; pressing the shift key or caps lock slows down the untrained typist. However, the children did use upper case letters when it suited them and they did have to press the shift key to make exclamation marks. So why did they make capitals in some instances but not in others? Distinctiveness attracts. Visual effects were a way of drawing attention, either to demonstrate playfulness or individuality (e.g. 'Oh Ma GoD Ur PaGeS R WICkEd') or to create salience (e.g. 'THANKS FOR STICKY').

Full stops were notable by their infrequency. The sentence, fundamental to formal writing, was largely redundant in this social milieu. If e-messages are taken to be speech-like, the omission of full stops may also imply the possibility of continuation in ongoing conversation as graphic utterance and response (see also Ella's transcript in Chapter 7). There were no commas at all in this sample of 28 stickies. Apostrophes as a means of showing possession and omission were entirely absent (e.g.

'hi! my names sophie!'). Question marks were either omitted or substituted with exclamation marks (e.g. 'I'm bored! r u' and 'How did u get the background!'). Exclamation marks were rife. One of their functions was to give salience; they marked the remarkable (e.g. 'Hi Nic i just seen your bro!'). In combination with speech-like lexis and syntax (e.g. 'I'm back online now!'), they might also suggest orality by hinting at, but not specifying, intonation, intensity and rhythm, whether read out audibly or performed in the receiver's head. On occasions when club members made new contacts (e.g. 'hi! my names sophie!'), responded to a recently made contact (e.g. 'Hay Nic! U can make your own pic now'), or re-contacted people they knew well (e.g. 'Hi Nics!'), they suggest the affective and the attitudinal associated with befriending, friendliness and friendship. There is not necessarily a one-to-one correspondence between a single signifier and a single meaning. Functionalities such as indicating surprise, invoking orality and marking an un-school-like environment are not mutually exclusive and can be co-present in the signification of a single exclamation mark.

Where did these practices come from, and how were they established? Framed by explicit rules devised to ensure safe and respectful exchange, the children were able to decide on the content, register and graphic appearance of their contributions. Over time certain semiotic practices had become regularized. The children did not invent texting-like writing or speech-like chat. Its origins derived from wider social practices. Texting on mobile devices has become established with astounding speed, in part in response to the limitations of the medium—three letters ascribed to each button and the limited space of the screen. Recognizing its common use in informal exchange, it was adopted for its aptness to this computer-mediated social network. Generated within the club, it was accepted and sustained through the social interactions of its members. This was a child-initiated collective construction of what messaging was. Socially responsive and socially dynamic, the regularized design of the e-notes shaped, confirmed, sustained and proliferated the club's practices.

The provisionality of digital writing allows children to experiment with the semiotics of presentation. In their use of word processors and presentation software, children readily avail themselves of typographic options which change the visuality of writing. They can be observed deliberating, sometimes for apparently inordinate lengths of time, over font, size, weight (e.g. plain, bold), style (e.g. italicizing, shadow, outline) and colour—and a source of some anxiety for teachers who are concerned about subject matter rather than its graphic appearance. These choices are not trivial. Typographical resources provide ways of making meaning beyond wording (Stockl, 2005; Van Leeuwen, 2005b; Waller, 1996). For example, selecting an 'old-fashioned' font was a metaphor for locating *Alice in Wonderland* historically (Matthewman and Triggs, 2004: 127–128). Graphic appearance is meaningful.

Contemporary computer-generated written text has a standardized appearance irrespective of whose fingers tap the keys: in uniformity of lettering, spacing between letters, words and lines, and the size and 'look' of different fonts. It precludes the individuality of handwriting. Typographical plainness is entirely usual in digital messaging, and is characterized by lack of variation in colour, font or emphasis. It is not that this preset visuality is meaningless, but that its very routine-ness represents the 'good enough' of speedy composition and sending. As with texting on a mobile phone, typographic resources in sticky messaging were not available at the click of a button in toolbar menus. Scrolling text could be programmed, and, with the required skills, images could be added:

> 'If you manage to do it right you can put pictures on or moving words that go through the screen then disappear and then they come back on again.'

'Managing to do it right' was not without challenge, and demanded access to certain technological know-how. From what children said, moving writing and image attract attention and interest, and are associated with fun, humour, motivation and engagement. The very presence of adjustments to the visuality of writing may also have been a demonstration of technological skill, and hence a display of identity. Since this took significant time and effort, it slowed down the process of composition, reduced the pace of sending and decreased the rate and volume of communicational exchange. As a consequence, children sometimes stylized the ordinariness of the default plain black typography with symbols available on the keyboard, such as a preceding and succeeding swung dash embellishment to create a pleasing visual symmetry. Selection of sticky background colour (pink, green, blue or yellow) was a choice the children relished. This variety gave scope for individual preference quickly and with ease.

Taken as design, writing consists of an array of semiotic features. Writing practices not only shape which lexical choices are made and how they are put together (e.g. voice, modality and clausality), but also how the resources of spelling, punctuation, typography or orthography, layout and materiality are deployed. Choice is a process of selecting from alternatives. This presupposes that there are alternatives from which to choose. Some choices are mutually exclusive. What is not chosen can be as significant as what is (e.g. 'hi' or 'hey' in preference to 'hello', and manifestly avoiding the formality of 'Dear' or 'To'). Choices are made in relation to other choices. Each choice and combination of choices is meaningful. Design is not a case of moving sequentially from word choice to syntactical constructions to layout. These essential components of writing become melded in the graphic product as a semiotic ensemble, and they are either co-generated simultaneously or produced in quick succession in the act of writing. One sign co-functions with another, and the semiotic interrelationships of sign complexes subsist in single words and across the full text. As she directed a question to a teacher moderator in synchronous chat, Siobhan's question 'pete wat skool da ya teach' (in formal writing 'Pete, in which school do you teach?') was a deliberate avoidance of the conventions of formal writing, in terms of syntax, spelling and punctuation. Together, these intensify the informality of the exchange.

Language has 'functional plurality' (Halliday, 1978: 56) as subject matter and social relations—the 'ideational' and the 'interpersonal'—are 'mapped' (ibid.: 50) onto one another 'to form a single integrated structure' (ibid.: 128) which represent 'simultaneous configurations of meanings of different kinds' (ibid.: 136). Mia suddenly found herself alone as one lunch-time chat session came to an end:

13:03 p.m.	any1 there ccoooooooooooooeeeeeeeeeee!!!!!!!!!!!!!!!!
13:03 p.m.	g2g c ya l8tr
13:04 p.m.	any1 there
13:05 p.m.	c u xxxxxxxxxxxxxx

In combining texting-like spelling and abbreviation ('any1' for 'anyone'; 'g2g' for 'got to go'; 'c ya l8r' for 'see you later'; and 'c u' for 'see you'), all in lower case, along with 'x' to carry the affective, it is not that one semiotic resource is restricted to the social and another to subject matter. Sign making is far more complex than this. This holds back any opposition of the 'what' of the 'ideational' and the 'who for' of the 'interpersonal' (Halliday, 1978) existing independently of the resources that realize them. Plurality of meaning is combined in discrete graphic features and multiplied in sign complexes.

Being a good writer shifts. Even within the classroom, what writing is changes (e.g. the language and layout of a poem as against a report). This is also the case with drawing. As children move between subjects of the curriculum, scope for expressiveness in art contrasts with the dispassionate diagrams of science or technical plans, historical timelines with the symbols of geographical maps. Children develop 'a repertoire of different drawings systems and an incipient knowledge of how each is powerful' (Wolf and Perry, 1988: 22). On the other hand, in addition to deep-seated distinctions, there are also certain continuities. This is a warning against setting up 'false dichotomies' (Hull and Schultz, 2001: 577) between representational practices. One graphic text is in many respects like another, yet quite different. With remarkable alacrity, children learn what is what. Their capacity for responding to different design demands is quite astounding. Conversely, 'getting it wrong' is testimony to the complexity of interpreting sometimes subtle shifts in text-making practices.

Un-school-like practices construct particular kinds of texts and particular kinds of literacy (Burnett et al., 2006; Merchant, 2005). With astonishing creativity and apparent ease suggesting 'an enormous fund of specialized knowledge' (Smith, 1984), the sticky messagers integrated complexly interrelated signs apt to social relations in the club in a seamlessly interwoven but understated semiotic orchestration. Whilst undoubtedly drawing on their curricular learning in literacy lessons, in selecting and combining semiotic resources these children created something very different from formal school writing. But did they write and read with confidence, fluency and understanding? Did they demonstrate imagination, inventiveness and critical awareness? This depends on how these qualities are defined and where they are looked for. From a social semiotic perspective, these e-messages are entirely literate within the practices of the social environment of the club in and for which they were designed. It is not that this kind of writing is inferior, but rather that its criteria for sufficiency differ because of the social environment. The design of writing for informal purposes would not be apt to the more formal environment of school, and formal writing would appear incongruous or a sign of inexperience in an informal context. Un-school-like writing is not inadequate, nor is school writing necessarily 'right' or 'better'.

It is not that there is one definitively 'right' way of writing, and that other forms are mere corruptions. Always situated within the discourses of particular social groups or networks, literacy practices epitomize certain values and viewpoints rather than others, varying according to beliefs, identities, lifestyles, genders, ethnicities, and so on, which are embedded in relations of power and realized in particular rules, structures and procedures (Barton, Hamilton and Ivanic, 2000; Gee, 1996; Street, 1984). It is not at all that developing a rich vocabulary, learning to create varied syntactical constructions and being able to spell and punctuate confidently in ways apt to the different genres of formal writing are not important. As a society, we want young people to have access to the resources that enable them to write with assurance for a range of formal purposes. Even so, experience of different kinds of writing is not necessarily detrimental to formal literacy learning, but rather 'can genuinely expand existing repertoires' (Moss, 2001: 110). Casual exchange between children is important for learning how to interact in the everyday world, and to being a citizen in contemporary, increasingly globalized, societies. Children are not just writers-in-waiting preparing for the representational and communicational work of the future. They are agentive text makers in the here and now.

'GETTING IT WRONG' IN COMMUNCATIONAL INTERACTION

Communicative exchange is imagined in the process of making and actualized at the moment of receipt. Based on existing social relations, messagers envision the person or people for whom the communication is intended and shape their designs accordingly. Although a message becomes a 'fulfilled' communication only when read and interpreted by the recipient, the maker anticipates understanding from its very inception. This shaping of meaning challenges the notion of 'egocentricism' (Piaget, 1929), which contends that children are aware of the world only from their own perspective. Kathleen (age 6 years) created her email message for her uncle with the aim of clarity, anticipating unimpaired comprehension. She announced the good news that she had 'got a new baeg' the week previously (Figure 4.1a).

Sometimes, 'getting it wrong' emerges through interaction with others. In online messaging—as in sending and receiving a letter or a postcard—the writer and reader are not physically co-present in the act of writing and reading. The moment of exchange is bodily distanced. Absent at the moment of delivery, Kathleen's control over her uncle's interpretation was relinquished. On receipt, Martin was placed in a position of uncertainty. Despite Kathleen's principled design, a communicational hiccup occurred where a particular meaning had been intended. The word that provided the key to understanding the whole was an alternative spelling and therefore proved difficult to decipher. What is a 'baeg'? Settling on what seemed to be the most likely interpretation, Martin assumed that she had mis-spelt the word 'bag' (Figure 4.1b). When she received her uncle's reply, Kathleen realized that there had been a hitch in the exchange of meaning. Tracing back the origin of this misunderstanding to her spelling of the key word in her message, she sought to redress the situation by designing a response that would remove any further risk of misapprehension. Having consulted her mother about spellings (this was the first her parents knew about the exchange), she corrected unequivocally her uncle's reading: not a bag but a badge (Figure 4.1c).

Historical assimilation, adaptation and borrowing have resulted in English spelling being 'messy and indeterminate' (Halliday, 1989: 24). Children

---

hey   this kathleen. martin I have some very good news last week I got a
new baeg

4.1a   Kathleen's initiation.

So glad to hear you got a new bag. What kind is it and what colour?

Uncle Martin

4.1b   Martin's first reply.

---

survival 1 badge kathleen

4.2c   Kathleen's response.

CONGRATULATIONS   ON   YOUR   SWIMMING   SELF-SURVIVAL
BADGE!!!!   I WAS 11 BEFORE I GOT MINE. HOW OLD ARE YOU
NOW? HOW FAR CAN YOU SWIM? AND WHAT IS YOUR FAVOURITE
STROKE? LOVE UNCLE MARTIN

4.1d   Martin's second reply.

Figure 4.1   Email exchange between Kathleen and Martin.

have to learn complex spelling rules, as well as the irregularities of exceptions to patterns. Young writers are often faced with the uncertainty of the unfamiliar, and they are constantly resourceful in making the most of the resources they have at their disposal. Embodied knowledge—knowledge people have without recourse to information sources beyond themselves—is critical for making texts efficiently in the everyday world. Kathleen's spelling of 'baeg' may not be a conventionally correct version of 'badge', but it signifies serious semiotic effort. She knew that 'g' in the presence of 'e' can sound like 'j'. Alphabetic scripts have well-developed means by which phonemes can be represented as graphemes, but there are transitions between them. The 'distinctive features' of speech also include shifts between voicelessness and voicing; the energy of sounds and the force of breath; stresses, prolongations, shortenings and overlaps; tones and qualities; continuities and breaks—and these are complexly interrelated and variant (Jakobson and Halle, 1956). Kathleen's positioning of an 'e' between the 'b' and 'j' is a sensible graphic transcription of the aurality of the spoken form of 'badge'. Even if not formally correct, her spelling is principled.

In the two-way process of interactional exchange, online messaging is dialogue co-constructed in a series of production (initiation-as-message), interpretation (of that message) and response (a reply that connects with the preceding message(s) in the series). Some elements may taken up and developed whilst others might be ignored and dropped. Kathleen responded to her uncle's enquiry about type in 'survival 1 badge'—entirely justified since the signifier 'badge' did not specify what kind it was—but ignored his question about its colour, presumably because she considered this to be immaterial. Each message remains separate in that it was created by a different person, at a different time, in a different location and in different circumstances, yet is semiotically interwoven within the communicational chain as a whole. There was a sequential flow of graphic utterance and response as each of the participants took account of the message they had received and created a reply apt to the unfolding of the exchange. The final series is a jointly created design.

How 'getting it wrong' is handled varies according to the social environment. Evaluation and response are always there, and they are managed differently according to social relations. Unlike the representational experience of the largely solitary and unilateral writing of the classroom where teachers identify and mark 'mistakes', this 'misspelling' was negotiated in the etiquette of two-way communicational exchange between members of an extended family.

> 'Children are not simply 'socialized' by their involvement in family rules and structures; the family order is an arena of action whose rules and structures themselves represent resources which children competently manipulate in dealing with others' agendas and working out their own' (Hutchby and Moran-Ellis, 1998: 18).

Sensitive to his niece's feelings, Martin's second reply made no reference to the misunderstanding, but rather congratulated her and sought to sustain the exchange (Figure 4.1d). He did not inform her directly that she had made a mistake. An independent social agent, she was resourceful in evaluating, analysing, weighing up and resolving a communicational snag in her lived experience. In this nuanced interchange, Kathleen learned that digression from standardized spelling can be hazardous. An early childhood experience such as this is formative of learning not only with regard to spelling, but also in handling unforeseen hurdles in everyday communicational exchange.

Arrangement is unavoidable in spatial texts. Drawn and written items have to be positioned somehow in the space of the graphic surface and in relation to one other. Spatiality offers possibilities for covering and for leaving uncovered. There is meaning in marking, and there is also meaning in not marking. So-called 'white space' does not alter how the signifiers of writing or drawing appear, unlike presentational resources such as letter case, typography, size or animation. It becomes meaningful relative to its amount within and between graphic items, and its distribution across the full text. In writing, the size of gaps between letters and groups of letters and absence of gaps in joined script indicate the discreteness of words. Embedded in contemporary writing, we are barely aware of this; it is what we do and what we expect. It was not always thus. In Anglo Saxon England, writing was graphically continuous in that it consisted of an uninterrupted stream of evenly spaced letters or *scripto continua* (Parkes, 1991: xvi). Seventh century Irish scribes first introduced gaps between words in their copies of Latin manuscripts in response to the needs of a readership for whom this Romance language was unlike their own (ibid.: 1–4). Separation is a means of framing that creates boundaries between lexical items. Regular spacing between the evenly sized and proportioned lettering of words is a teaching objective for 5- to 7-year-olds (DfEE and QCA, 1999: 49), and is generally well established during the first year of formal schooling.

In accordance with the writing practices of formal genres, Kathleen variously omitted and inserted gaps between letters in order to show words as discrete entities. However, on two occasions she made double spaces and once she created a triple space (Figure 4.2a). The outcome is consistent spacing between some words and irregularities between others. Why did she do this and what might it mean? One response might be that she 'got it wrong'. Another explanation could be that the action of pressing the space bar is automized, and therefore devoid of meaning. This raises questions around whether it is acceptable to recognize only certain semiotic features and to background, even disregard, others, or to construe them as meaningless. If features of writing are discounted because they lie beyond that which is commonly valued, the semiotic plenitude of design is overlooked. Assuming that text making is principled, why did she do this?

Kathleen's spacing is varied, but it is not at all random. Considered in relation to her wording, about which more is known than arrangement and in relation to which it subsists, possible explanations begin to emerge. Three taps of the space bar after the opening word 'hey' create a particular visual effect. Separated from what comes next, the greeting occupies a discrete space. Similarly, three taps of the space bar before 'this kathleen' and two taps after it create a frame around this graphic unit. Visually conspicuous, this separates Kathleen's self-identification from that which comes before and after. If the variation in distancing is equalized by imposing single spaces between each word, and if the full stop is also removed, the result is that the named subject ceases to stand out (Figure 4.2b). Kathleen's self-naming then becomes visually undifferentiated from the regularity of the surrounding words. Her full stop (the only punctuation mark in her message) and double space together create a 'new section' boundary. They mark the end of the greeting and self-identification, and the start of the email's main subject matter. The effect is a fleeting moment of anticipation as the reader awaits what is to come next: a question, a reminder, a surprise, a request, a joke? With one further exception, there are consistent single spaces between words in the remainder of the message. Kathleen chunked together the email's main subject matter as one graphic unit: 'I have some very good news last week I got a new'. Spelling 'baeg' was apparently a challenging moment that required some considered reflection. The double spacing between 'new' and 'baeg' may represent a brief moment of hesitation or indeed a relatively prolonged period of thought before committing letters to the screen. Alternatively, Kathleen may have considered a double space important before typing the message's key word. Whatever, the outcome was that the key word 'baeg' was moved into its own space. Capital letters and full stops indicate sentence boundaries in the formal writing of school. Kathleen's email is not sentenced. She created visual blocks. Principled, her chunking shows different components of her message, each of which is a segment of meaning: she greets; she identifies herself; she calls for the named receiver's attention and announces that information of significant import is forthcoming; and she withholds her

---

hey---this-kathleen.--martin-I-have-some-very-good-news-last-week-I-got-
a-new--baeg

4.2a   Kathleen's spacing (taps of the space bar shown as dashes).

---

hey this kathleen martin I have some very good news last week I got a
new baeg

4.2b   Imposed single spacing.

Figure 4.2   Spacing.

surprise right until the last word. Kathleen showed connection and disconnection through proximity and distance. Spacing is a vital feature in the
semiotic plenitude of her message.

Kathleen's message is speech-like—a feature well documented in studies
of email (e.g. Ferrara, Brunner and Whittemore, 1991; Jarvis, Hargreaves
and Comber, 1997; Merchant, 2003). Her expectation might have been that
intonation, rhythm, intensity and phrasing, whilst absent orthographically,
would be added performatively in her uncle's reading of her message. If so,
Kathleen's graphic spacing could be a semiotic device to indicate temporal
spacing in that different sizing of spaces on the screen can serve as a metaphor for different lengths of time. Taken as speech-like, the two larger gaps
between her three blocks of writing might represent the pauses between the
'bursts' typical of the one-breath 'idea units' (Chafe, 1982: 37) or 'information units' (Halliday, 1989: 54–55) of talk. In conversation, silence is a
semiotic resource that shows disconnection and gives space for response.
Due to the asynchronicity of email, the message maker is required to fill
this graphic gap with ongoing writing.

Can omission of spacing between words also be principled, or is it just
plain wrong? In an email to her grandmother, Laurel (age 8 years) created
the subject caption 'Christmascoming'. In a literacy lesson, this might be
deemed incorrect on two counts: a word and spacing are apparently missing. In speech, the present indicative 'is' would not be enunciated as a separate articulation but would be elided, hence not 'Christmas is coming' but
'Christmas's coming'. Doubling the 's' would not work ('Christmassscom-
ing'). A similar thing happens in 'this kathleen.' This could have been a slip.
In the excitement of the moment or the sheer speed of creating and sending,
Kathleen could have forgotten to repeat the last two letters of 'this' to make
the verb. As imagined speech made graphically, the contraction 'this' is a
precise transcription of 'this's'. Laurel showed the absence of a temporal
gap in speech by removing the spatial gap in writing, just like the omission
of spaces between words with a close syntactical connection in the manuscripts made by Irish scribes in the first half of the eighth century (Parkes,
1991: 4). This condensation was not a mistake, although it might be unacceptable in formal writing. It was a graphic remaking of a phrase as said
and heard, and shaped by Laurel as a single graphic unit. This fulfilled her
aim for a concise subject caption. It is entirely principled.

Power relations are realized in the smallest micro act and they shift with
context. Kathleen's decision not to respond to her uncle's second message
put an end to the series. Ignoring teacher questioning would have been an
act of subordination, a refusal to comply—and with consequential reper-
cussions. Discontinuation of the series was a sign of Kathleen's power. Furthermore, as the initiator of the exchange, she assumed control in making
certain decisions. In the classroom, teachers instruct when texts are made,
and what kind. Kathleen's decision to email her uncle one Sunday evening
at 17:03 p.m. was entirely her own, and her sending and receiving of a

series of four messages over a period of four days was undertaken quite autonomously at home using her own account. Her choice of email defined the mode—writing—which she clearly considered adequate to her needs. This had implications for the kinds of signs she could make, and for the mode in which she expected her uncle to reply. It shaped the design of their exchange.

'GETTING IT WRONG' IN THE CLASSROOM

How 'getting it wrong' in writing and drawing is handled varies according to the roles and relations of everyday social interaction. In the well-established practices of school, attention is drawn to 'mistakes' in a very direct way. This may also be the case at home and beyond when a parent, sibling or carer takes on a pedagogic role. In this ideological frame, it is not that directness is synonymous with want of sensitivity or lack of courtesy, but that it can be an immediate, effective and efficient means of providing feedback. Schoolwork frequently entails completion of graphic tasks that are designed to test knowledge and understanding of foregoing learning activities experienced by the class, and to provide opportunities to demonstrate attainment of subject knowledge, understanding and skills. Not achieving these targets can be seen as failure to engage or lack of ability. Sometimes children excel, sometimes they 'get it right' or 'nearly right', and sometimes 'wrong' or 'badly wrong'. What if this is looked at again?

Some signifiers are restricted largely, if not entirely, to specialized domains (e.g. certain mathematical, chemical and phonetic symbols). Others are encountered, interpreted and made in a variety of social environments. Arrows are semiotic resources that most children have come across in their lives beyond school as well as in their classroom experience. Their occurrences on notices in the everyday environment show where to go or point out items of interest. In either case, they indicate direction and movement: of the whole body in where to go or of the eyes in where to look. On construction toy instruction sheets, arrows indicate what should go with what, and where. As 'vectors' (Kress and Van Leeuwen, 2006), they are a means of creating relationships between graphic items. In non-fiction texts, arrows can perform a narrative or 'conceptual' function by indicating actional processes, transformations and changes over time (ibid.: 63–70).

Following on from teaching, hypothesizing (see Chapter 6) and hands-on investigation in a lesson on magnetic force, the challenge now facing the class was to record the movements as well as the outcomes of attraction and repulsion on the fixity of the page: the 'what happened when...' of the worksheet (Figure 4.3). What is significant is that use of arrows was stipulated, but their graphic form was assumed. The teacher used his fingers to suggest straightness and a horizontal orientation (Table 4.2). These properties were not mentioned in speech. By enacting converging and

Table 4.2 Representing Arrows Actionally (Teacher)

	Speech	Gesture at upper body height	
a)	*how are you going to show that they moved towards each other? what could you use? Tom?*		from a distance, brings his index fingers towards one another on *moved*
b)	*arrows* (Tom)		
c)	*yes well done you could use arrows*		
d)	*so you could draw a picture of two bar magnets stuck together*		shapes his index fingers and thumbs to represent the outline of the magnets and moves his hands forwards and backwards slightly
e)	*with arrows*		points his index fingers inwards towards each other and makes a forwards and backwards motion
f)	*showing that they've stuck together*		shapes his index fingers and thumbs to represent the outline of the magnets and makes slight forwards and backwards movements
	Enacts the processes of attraction and repulsion with the actual bar magnets and provides the scientific terminology.		
g)	*use arrows to show what's happening*		
h)	*so if they're pulling towards each other*		holding the magnets in his palms, brings his straight and pointed index fingers inwards towards each other from a distance

Continued

Table 4.2   Continued

i)	*the arrows are going to go in aren't they?*		moves (now close) index fingers in a slight backwards and forwards movement, then rests with the magnets touching and his index fingers parallel
j)	*outwards because they're pushing away from each other*		elbows tight to body, makes an effortful enactment of pulling apart the magnets

opposing motion simultaneously with spoken verbs and adverbs such as 'moved', 'pulling', 'towards each other' and later 'outwards [...] pushing away from each other', the teacher modelled the potentiality for arrow signifiers to carry the meaning of movement and directionality. Simulating the outline shape of the magnets with his index fingers and thumbs and later holding the actual objects whilst 'miming' the properties of arrows was a way of implying a relationship between arrows and representations of magnets.

Variations in the form of arrows across the 27 texts are surprising in their diversity: straight and curved; vertical, horizontal and diagonal; separate and crossed; shorter and longer; single and overlaid shaft lines; V-shaped, triangular and filled heads; single-headed and double-headed; singly and in pairs; close and distant; positioned between and above drawings of magnets. In 16 texts (59 per cent), arrows indicate movement—and in a whole range of ways. Of the 40 instances of arrows depicting motion, 82.5 per cent are positioned in the space between two representations of magnets. This indicates the area where the movement happened. As the two magnets moved in opposite directions simultaneously, identical but reversed arrows show how this magnet is attracted towards that and that towards this, or how one is repelled from another (e.g. Figure 4.3a). This was later explained:

Di: And what else have you done?
Tom: The arrows so you can see they're connected together.
Di: And what about these (*indicating repulsion in Question 3*)?
Tom: The north pole and the north pole are together so that they push out.
Di: So how did you show that?
Tom: I showed that by using the arrows again.

Di:	And what's the difference between the arrows?
Tom:	This arrow's gone inwards and this one's gone outwards.

The ends of Tom's arrow shafts and the points of his arrowheads touch the facing inner edges of his representations of bar magnets to show attraction and repulsion respectively. In order to show attraction, Rohana positioned two identical arrows in opposing directionalities one above the other in the gap between her representations of magnets (Figure 4.3b). Arguably, Tom focused on the objects and indicated their point of movement towards or away from one another, whilst Rohana focused on the space covered by the objects in moving. Both do the job, but with subtle shifts in what each child attended to. There is more than one way of 'getting it right'.

What about use of arrows that are seemingly ambiguous? Positioning outwardly pointing arrows at each outer end of representations of bar magnets is an apt way of indicating the motion of repulsion (Figure 4.3c). So why did Dean also add smaller inwardly pointing arrows in between? Indeed, he repeated these two pairs of arrows in the subsequent question that asked about juxtaposing two south poles. He knew that like poles repel. During class exchange, in response to a question posed by his teacher, Dean replied, 'If you have two of the same colours that push they won't connect.' Assuming that what he did was what he intended, the most likely explanation is that the smaller, inner pair depicts the experimental method of moving the magnets together (see Table 6.1f–g) and the larger outer arrows show the scientific process of pushing apart.

What about when children 'get it nearly right' or 'not quite right but on the right lines'? During whole-class teaching, Lily demonstrated her engagement with the terminology of forces:

> Two bar magnets are placed horizontally with opposite poles facing on the visualiser and projected onto the class screen. 'Look,' the teacher says. He moves the magnets closer together by pushing on each end with his index fingers, and they come together with a click. There is silence. The teacher looks at the class. 'What force is acting between them? Not a push (..)'—he raises his fists to neck height and brings them together—'because they're coming together. It's a (..)? Lily?' Lily replies, 'Pull.' 'It is a pull. Well done!'

Like other children, Lily represented the attractive movement of each magnet towards the other by filling the space between her drawings of magnets with arrows in an above / below positioning and extending the full width of the space (Figure 4.3d). However, she made arrows in a converging directionality to represent repulsion. Why did she do this? One explanation is that she got it wrong. Taking seriously what she inscribed in her worksheet and what she said may offer an alternative interpretation:

2. Draw what happened when a north pole was placed towards a south pole.

Opposite poles ~~Repel~~ **Attract** .

3. Draw what happened when a north pole was placed towards another north pole.

Like poles *Repel* .

4.5a   Tom.

2. Draw what happened when a north pole was placed towards a south pole.

Opposite poles A++ract .

3. Draw what happened when a north pole was placed towards another north pole.

Like poles repel .

4.5b   Rohana.

2. Draw what happened when a north pole was placed towards a south pole.

Opposite poles Vepel .

3. Draw what happened when a north pole was placed towards another north pole.

4.5c   Dean.

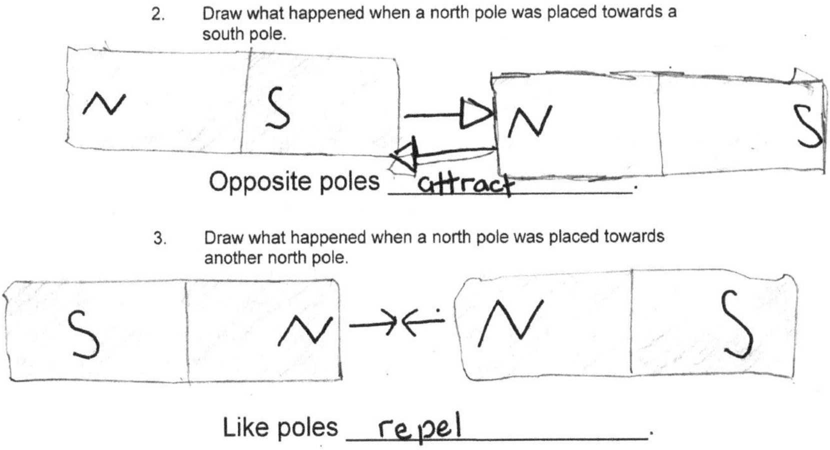
2. Draw what happened when a north pole was placed towards a south pole.
N
S
N
S
Opposite poles attract.
3. Draw what happened when a north pole was placed towards another north pole.
S
N
N
S
Like poles repel.

4.5d Lily.

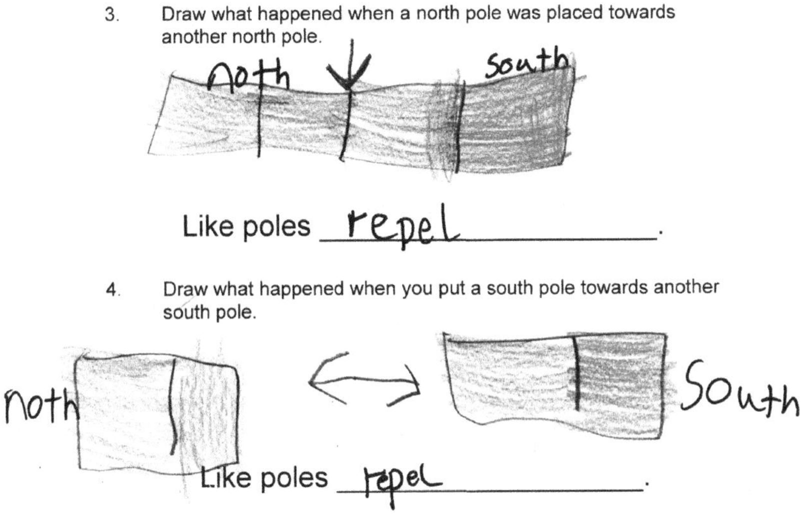
3. Draw what happened when a north pole was placed towards another north pole.
noth
South
Like poles repel.
4. Draw what happened when you put a south pole towards another south pole.
noth
South
Like poles repel.

4.5e Yadin.

Figure 4.3 Showing magnetic force with arrows.

Di: Can you explain how you did your arrows Lily (*referring to attraction in Question 2*)?

Lily: Well the one on the left side has the arrow going to the right side and the on the right side has the arrow going to the left side.

Di: And what does that show?

Lily: That they're going that way and sticking together.

Di: And what about the bottom two (*referring to repulsion in Questions 3 and 4*)?

Lily: The bottom two (..) 'cos they were both the same side like north and north and south and south (.) you just did two arrows (..) that means not sticking together.

In her representation of attraction and in her related explanation, the triangular tips of her arrowheads indicate very precisely the point of meeting, i.e. where the two sides of each of the two bar magnets will touch. Indeed, she erased and re-drew the lower arrowhead in order to make its point touch the inner end of the left-hand magnet drawing. Carried through to showing repulsion, the bumping up of the two arrowheads—the touching of their tips—may be a way of indicating a point of not-meeting, with the area of white space in between showing separation. Even if unconventional, this would be entirely principled.

What about when representation slips over into 'getting it plain wrong'? Yadin's naming of the process ('repel', which, along with 'attract', was written on the board) is scientifically correct, as is his labelling (Figure 4.3e). By no means the only instance across the worksheets, his colouring is scientifically incorrect. Prohibition of shading until the 'real' work had been completed concurs with the commonly held notion that colouring is a mere time-filler:

> 'You can used coloured crayons to colour in your magnets (..) when you've finished all the writing and everything's ready (.) then you can go back and colour the poles if you like.'

For children who are still becoming accustomed to the new terminology of 'north and south poles', colouring as a primary means of differentiating the two sides of a bar magnet, rather than an add-on or an aesthetically pleasing luxury, might have provided a more straightforward route. Even so, why did Yadin conjoin to indicate repulsion, and why did he use a single downwardly pointing arrow? His explanation in the group interview went:

Di: Do you want to say anything Yadin? (..) look (.) you did an arrow here (*indicating his response to the third question*) tell me about that one.

Yadin: This arrow's going be down (.) means they going be join (..) that's straight.

Hollie: That one's supposed to be joined and that one's supposed to be apart and then they split apart.

Di: So what's that arrow again Yadin?

Yadin: That says straight arrow.

Di: And why is it a straight arrow?

Yadin: Because I have no space or (.) or (...) I don't know.

Hollie: He should have done it (.) 'cos he should have done the third one (.) draw what happened when a north pole faced towards another north pole.

Yadin: Rub out (*simultaneously*)
Yadin: I don't mind (.) it's rub out (.) they going be join (..) and that arrow's (.) see the arrow's going to be straight side (...) but I rub out.

Yadin appeared to be torn between justifying his response that 'they going be join' and his persistent contention that this arrow is 'straight' and 'straight side', and erasing it in order to conform to what was insisted by a classmate to be the correct answer. Pushing the issue in what seemed to be, for him, a vulnerable position appeared to me unethical, and so I did not pursue this further. Might there be other ways of accounting for this 'mistake'? Apparently straightforward, this worksheet proved to be demanding for the class, and not one was fully 'correct'. It could be that individuals had not grasped the scientific fact that like poles repel. Alternatively, it may have been that their interest was elsewhere when they completed the worksheet. During this part of the lesson the children were simultaneously pursuing other agendas as they socialized and 'played around'. It may also have been that children, many of whom spoke English as a second language, did not have the resources available to them to follow the lesson or to complete the worksheet.

Another possibility is that, with the procedural approach adopted for the investigation, facing like poles can result in attraction. In demonstrating how to complete this worksheet question, using the visualiser the teacher brought together two north poles. When he let go, the repelling force caused one of the magnets to rotate, and this resulted in an attractive force. There was delighted laughter from the class, and this occurrence was a theme that re-emerged in the interviews, indicating its salience for the children, such as Amira's comment:

> 'The visualiser helped us look at the magnets and remind us of how they thingy (.) stick together (..) and what they do if you hold the two sides together of the magnet and then you let go (.) then one of them twisters around.'

During hands-on investigation, Lauren, paired with Yadin, experienced a similar force:

> Lauren holds two magnets horizontally at head height, as her teacher had done in his earlier elicitation. Nothing happens. Her partner, Yadin, tells her that she has to put them together. Lauren replies 'I am' and positions them horizontally apart on the table, with the red ends towards each other, matching what is still displayed on the visualiser screen. As she pushes them closer, in accordance with the teacher's previous gestural instruction, the bar magnet to the left spins round and comes to rest on the edge of the table. As she touches it, it flicks round

suddenly and its blue end connects with the red end of the still magnet. Lauren looks at Yadin, eyes wide and mouth open.

This may have been the basis for ongoing disagreement in the interview:

Yadin: (???) straight one.
Hollie: But north and north can't go together (.) and south and south can't go together (.) and they won't go together.
Lauren: Yes they can.
Yadin: They can (???) try them.
Hollie: If north and north go together (.) and south and south go together (.) they will just push away.
Yadin: No they don't (.) no.
Lauren: No (.) but you like sticked it on the sides but not in the middle (..) you sticked it.

Yadin's 'straight side' may be his terminology for joining together the bar magnets lengthways during hands-on investigation which, in a similar way to the 'twister' seen on the visualiser and in Lauren's experimentation, resulted in an attractive force ('they going be join'). What is at first sight plain wrong might actually have been an endeavour to be exhaustive in representing all that he had observed in the lesson.

An important means by which children represent what they know, understand and can do in the everyday classroom, and a principal site for assessment, is their writing and, to a lesser extent, their drawing. Under the pressure to achieve curricular targets, it is important not to lose sight of the means to the end. If classroom text making is viewed as an opportunity for children to explore and experiment with the semiotic possibilities for representing their learning, then the effort they invest in their text making deserves to be valued. This is not a contention that they should always engage freely in open-ended activities, nor is it an argument against instruction. Rather, it is about taking time to ponder over what children have represented, and it shows respect for their efforts.

Even so, the origins of certain features of drawing and writing and the meanings associated with them may be inconclusive from texts alone. One recourse is dialogue around what was done and why. This can be illuminating. For example, the apparent anomaly of a cow drawn in a map on the theme of 'Computers in today's world' in the *Représentation* study was clarified in a subsequent interview when the child explained that it was actually a representation of a computer controlled milking system on his / her farm (Pearson and Somekh, 2003: 18–19). This is a reminder to take seriously the detail of children's texts and not to dismiss as 'incorrect' that which is not immediately obvious. Even so, teasing out why certain resources were chosen in preference to others may prove inconclusive because meanings are not necessarily fixed (see Chapter 3) or because individuals may not have certain explanatory resources available to them. Exploring with children the poten-tialities of semiotic resources and explicit discussion and modelling around the effects of different choices and combinations extends their availability to individuals, thereby offering expanded scope for representational choice. Recent research in England that calls for a rethinking of the weight and orga-nization of the curriculum and that suggests space for schools to respond to the communities they serve is promising in this regard (Alexander, 2010).

DISCUSSION

Criteria for the production of texts are highly particularized, and they shift. They vary according to what is being written or drawn and for whom. It fol-lows that any definition of sufficiency can only be provisional. Text making includes evaluation of what is needed here and now, and it is always socially specific. That which is apt to one environment may be unsuited to another. This requires adaptability. Certain configurations of drawing and writing are suited to certain situations and not to others. What can go unexplained or without elaboration in one instance may need to be realigned for some-one else somewhere else. When children respond in unexpected ways, this is not necessarily malfunction. Recognizing contextual variables is not always easy. Social environments can be confusing, even contradictory. This is why children sometimes make unintentional *faux pas* which can be interpreted by convention-laden adults as inappropriate, wrong or even impertinent. Through feedback from others along with reflection on the effectiveness of their text making, children learn that there are multiple, complex and some-times subtle contextual variables which make certain kinds of representation fitting to one situation and not necessarily to another.

The contention that we should strive to understand where children 'go wrong' is not an argument against the 'right' way of doing things. It is not that 'anything goes'. Within the framing of the curriculum, learning is specified and forms of representation are regularized; there are right and wrong ways of doing things. As a society, we want young people to develop the knowledge, skills and understanding, along with means of expression, that we consider to be important to being an educated citizen. Teachers are accountable to senior managers, external inspectors, parents, and of course, children in providing what is needed to attain the requirements of the curriculum. Even so, when children 'get it wrong', it does not necessarily follow that their text making is not principled. Dismissing out of hand that which falls outside what is expected may be a disservice. Showing respect for what children draw and write shifts the lens from failure, imperfection and deficiency to endeavouring to under-stand what they did and why. Recognizing the semiotic work children invest in their text making has implications for responding in ways that nurture positive dispositions.

5 'Jumble', Shorthand and Repetition

Sometimes, children's texts are neat and clearly ordered (e.g. Figure 1.1, Figure 2.3, and Figure 3.1a). Sometimes, they are apparently disorganized, even 'a mess'. What if texts that might at first sight appear to be a mass of confusion are looked at again? Repetition is a converse of the apparent chaos of diverse components. In school, children are often exhorted to use variety in their descriptive language and in their sentence beginnings, structures and connectives. Why do they sometimes repeat graphic items? Does similarity, even identicalness, necessarily indicate lack of imagination or limited ability? On occasion, children draw and write economically, omitting detail. Is this laziness? What if 'jumble', shorthand and repetition are examined as semiotic work?

'JUST A JUMBLE'

Layout is an unavoidable feature of the spatiality of graphic texts. There is greater scope for variation in the arrangement and presentational features of some genres than others. Web pages, posters, magazines, worksheets and non-fiction books, for example, are widely varied in terms of how different kinds of image and blocks of writing are presented and set out. Even around the age of 2 years, toddlers have at their disposal a range of means for organizing the space of the page with intentionality (Lancaster, 2007). Preschoolers are able to differentiate between and remake the graphic appearance of different kinds of texts such as the discrete areas of image and written instructions in a recipe (Kenner, 2000a: 73–75). By the time they reach the age of 9 or 10 years, children have encountered and made texts set out in a whole range of arrangements. In stories and reports, they often organize writing and drawing as discrete modal blocks in an above / below assemblage, and less often a side-by-side configuration (e.g. Millard and Marsh, 2001: 56–59). Sometimes, continuous written text flows around drawings or drawing partially protrudes into a block of writing (ibid.: 55, 59). In diagrams and posters, drawing and writing are more visually integrated (e.g. Bearne et al., 2004).

Modal loading shifts. As children encounter and make different kinds of texts at home and in school for a variety purposes, the balance between writing and image alters. Proportional coverage of the graphic area varies according to genre: sometimes writing predominates (e.g. stories), sometimes image takes up a greater amount of space (e.g. digital games), sometimes one or the other is entirely absent (e.g. photograph albums), and sometimes there is a more even balance (e.g. magazines and non-fiction books). Creating a synopsis that fits on one side of a page in 'concept' mapping (Novak and Gowin, 1984) or 'mind' mapping (Buzan, 1993) offers certain semiotic potentialities and imposes certain constraints. Key features of the topic are selected and expressed, as it were, in shorthand. This closes down the semiotic possibilities of continuous writing. However, a diagrammatic structure opens up options in the choice of single words or short phrases, arrangement (the organization of items in relation to one another and within the space of the graphic surface), relative scale (enlargement, diminution, equal sizing), framing (separating with white space or enclosing lines) and linkage (connecting lines with or without arrowheads).

Concept mapping is not new to the classroom. It is a means by which students can demonstrate, and teachers can assess, their knowledge and understanding of curricular subject matter, often in secondary and higher education science (e.g. Cifuentes and Hsieh, 2004; Kinchin, de Leij and Hay, 2005; Tekkaya, 2003). Until recently, the potential of mapping for the purposes of research has remained largely untapped. Rather than modifying erroneous conceptualization or promoting meaningful learning, the 'Computers in my world' maps generated for the ImpaCT2 evaluation were used as a means of accessing children's experience-informed knowledge and understanding of digital technologies in everyday life (Somekh et al., 2002).

With its 'jumble' of multiple links, George's map might appear to be 'just a mess' (Figure 5.1). In the scripted instructions, map makers were asked to 'draw lines between the drawings that you feel are linked'. George made a total of 70 links. Did he 'just go wild', joining items irrespective of where they went to and from? This is possible. An alternative is that his intention was to indicate multiple interconnections and complex interlinkage, elsewhere termed a 'net' (Kinchin and Hay, 2000: 47–48) or 'spaghetti' (Pearson and Somekh, 2003: 10–11). This alone would be purposeful and principled. Diagrammatic lines are a resource for constructing relationships. As labelling links—the 'propositions' of concept mapping (Novak and Gowin, 1984: 34–36)—was not a task requirement, the reasons for making connections did not have to be specified. Items might be 'like', 'connected to', 'give access to', 'be associated with', technologically, functionally, locationally, socially, and so on. There are clearly marked relations in George's multiple interconnections, even if these are interpretationally exacting: games are linked with games, workplaces are linked through email and the telephone, and a building contractor is linked with a hotel building. Meaningfulness replaces muddle.

So what about the clutter of nodes? Is their positioning purely random, with no attention to systematic arrangement? The request to make links as lines was explicit in the scripted instructions, but there was no specification, or even mention, of layout. Towards the top of the map, George drew himself ('me'). Arranged and linked in the closest positioning are connections with (presumably) home (an unlabelled house), three digital gaming devices (one linked twice), two named games and the computer. These nodes may represent what was most important to George within the framing of 'Computers in my world'. School, also linked to 'me', is

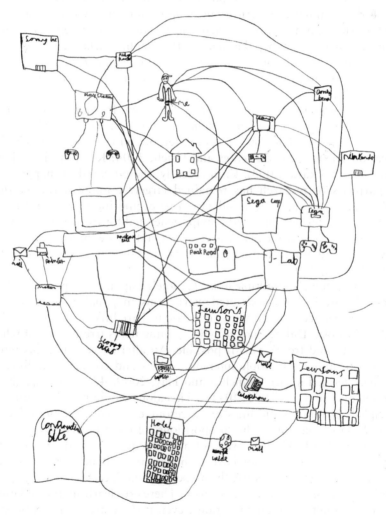

Figure 5.1 'Computers in my World' (George).

located further away towards the centre of the page. The wider community (commercial company, hotel and construction site) is more distant in its positioning towards the bottom of the map and is indirectly rather than directly linked to 'me'. Through his arrangement of nodes and linkage, George seems to be indicating widening spheres in relation to himself.

At first glance, Amy's map (she was in the same class of 9- and 10-year-olds as George) appears to be an apt selection of subject matter, but with nodes randomly bunched in something of a jumble around an enlarged, centrally positioned image (Figure 5.2). Is this 'just a muddle'? Closer examination reveals a classificatory structure. Amy arranged her map as four clusters, which Frances described as 'a family or something'. Four links emanating from the central node (excepting the one return link) have the role of bringing together dissimilar items which do not share likeness of form, but that are unified by other taxonomic characteristics. Amy grouped the 'what', the 'how', the 'why' and the 'where' of the topic of 'Computers in my world'. Items of equipment making up the 'kit' of a computer system occupy the right and extreme top right-hand areas of the page: connected to the monitor with its adjoined keyboard she made links to her drawings of a speaker (with its 'Music and noise' sub-association), a 'Disc Box' (not a box containing discs but a processing unit), a mouse and a printer (with a paper association). To the bottom right of the map are resources available on a computer: games, 'Work files', a spreadsheet, 'Log on Box' and 'finding the time' (analogue and digital). The nodes to the left of the page catalogue digital information and communication: the web (note the precision of the content, order and 'punctuation' of the school website address), email (here for leisure purposes), fax (oral communication via the telephone and written information shown on the adjacent page) and video (moving image). To the top centre of her map, are locations where computers can be found: office, living room and 'Primary computer room'. Around one week later, in a related writing task Amy identified the components making up a computer system in her first paragraph, followed by a second on use of the computer for various purposes such as email and games and how this entails resources such as CDs and saving files, whilst the third paragraph focuses on places where computers are used 'in homes, in offices, in school and all round the world'. When asked why she had linked the nodes in her map as she did Amy's explanation went:

> 'It was in sections (..) and then like on this half I've done what you can find on the computer like the keyboard and the speaker and all that (.) that one just went off there (..) and then I've done where you can find computers (..) and then saying how emails work because I've done a laptop and then world wide web and then emails and then going on to fax machines (..) and then what you can find in computers (.) like you can find the spreadsheets and work files and games and all that.'

The linearity of writing and speech impose a sequential order, whilst the spatiality of the map enabled Amy to show these classifications simultaneously.

This was not an isolated instance of grouping. Seven other maps in this class set of 25 (28%) exhibit similar, if partial, classifying characteristics such as Oliver's discrete cluster of digital games (Figure 5.3). Set apart as a 'family' at a distance from other nodes, they are only items to occupy the upper right of his map. Constructing connection and disconnection with the resource of white space can be intensified or weakened by adjusting its relative proportion (Van Leeuwen, 2005a: 6–23). By marshalling other resources in cohort, such as framelines, size and colour—which themselves can be variously weighted (e.g. heaviness of line, relative scale, contrast of shades)—separation can be increasingly intensified. Oliver also used lines to indicate his grouping. A single link to the central topic node and internal interlinkage create exclusivity that connects what is within and separates this from what is beyond:

> 'Well I was just linking them together to give a clearer view to somebody that's reading it (.) to say that these are all games and they're linked together (..) so the Nintendo™ is a game but the PlayStation®2 (.) if I connect it to it (.) they'll see that it is a game but it's a different type of make (..) somebody could think that's a video player couldn't they (.) if they didn't know what it was (..) that's why I linked them

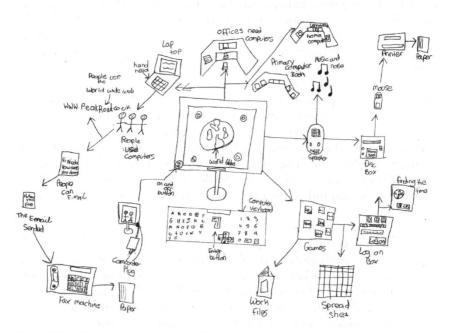

Figure 5.2 'Computers in my world' (Amy).

together (.) so if you know that one is a game (.) if you link them to-gether (.) the rest of them must be games.'

Similarities in detail (e.g. controls) unite items included in the grouping: 'Because like they're the same things almost.' Dissimilarities (e.g. the card and on-screen action) differentiate them: 'They would see the difference in the controls and that.' Justification of grouping was summarized as: 'They would all be in the same shop but apart from each other.' Oliver's co-deployment of the resources of layout, image detail and linkage to create an unambiguous classificatory grouping was principled.

'Reading pathways' (Kress and Van Leeuwen, 2006: 204–208) might be more or less insistent, more or less preferred. Across the full set of over 3,000 maps, a comparatively large and detailed node was frequently positioned in the centre of the page and surrounded with white space. From this, the majority of links 'radiate' outwards as in mind mapping (Buzan, 1993), rather than cascading hierarchically from top to bottom as in concept maps (Novak and Gowin, 1984). In response to the third question of the interview schedule—'Where did you start to draw and why did you start there?'—a number of children described their central node as 'the main thing' or 'really the first thing that came into my mind'. Prominence establishes the topic in focus, and it also constructs the 'entry conditions' for a preferred 'entry point' (Knox, 2007: 48). In a hub or radial—or a 'spoke' (Kinchin and Hay, 2000: 47) or 'one-centred' (Pearson and

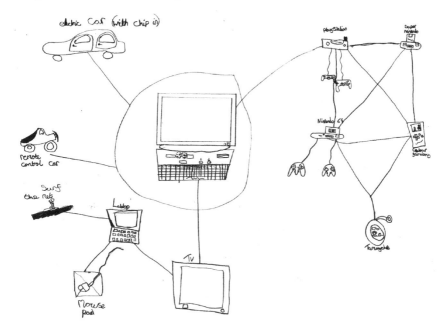

Figure 5.3 'Computers in my world' (Oliver).

Somekh, 2003: 10)—structure rather like a 'spider' diagram, exit from the nucleus is possible via any of the links (e.g. Figure 5.4). As theme and exposition, 'computerness' is in some sense shared by each of the linked exemplars. Once this structure has been recognized, the central node can be held as the given, with the repetitiousness of the radiating links releasing the map interpreter from the sort of careful tracking of each line that would be necessary with more complex interconnections such as George's (Figure 5.1). A methodical clockwise or anticlockwise 'reading' route is reasonable but not necessary, preferable or controllable, and there are numerous sequences in which these peripheral nodes might be viewed. Largely equal sizing of and distancing between them suppresses any suggestion of where to begin, or a patterned order to follow. Matched sizing, no central hub and complex interlinkage, such as George's map (Figure 5.1), leaves 'reading' pathways more open. This creates a non-hierarchical structure that suppresses a definitive entry point or a single directionality of 'reading'. Arguably, the computer to the centre left might be his intended starting point. It has the greatest number of links emanating from it (13 in total). However, due to the fairly even size and distancing between nodes, any might be chosen to begin exploring the map. There is no single beginning, centre or end. Amy's four classifications are grouped but not ranked. Largely equal size and equidistant distribution of nodes around the periphery of the page eliminates differential status (Figure 5.2). On the other hand, arrowheads indicate directionality, and may be intended to guide the order in which the nodes should be sequentially viewed within each section.

The design of 'reading' pathways shapes how the map 'reader' approaches, engages with and understands content (see also O'Toole, 1994). If the maps were to be reconfigured in an evenly sized and spaced linear sequence, they would lose features essential to their meaning. Hierarchies of salience are a means of guiding, driving, even compelling, ways of seeing. The sequence of 'reading' shapes how phenomena are attended to, thereby constructing how the 'reader' knows and understands. As well as the brief to communicate with a research audience, from what was said, diagrammatic structuring enabled the children to organize their interpretations of experience (e.g. 'I've put them in order like that (..) it's more neater to me') and assemblage was a way of constructing order and making sense for themselves (e.g. 'So really I used these to try and organize what I was going to actually use it for (.) and just so that I could understand'). The notions of 'externalizing concepts and propositions' (Novak and Gowin, 1984: 17) and the 'natural expression of Radiant Thinking' (Buzan, 1993: 55) presume that mapping is a means of making visible what is already inside people's heads. What these children said indicates that the process of selecting and combining resources in map making was itself a semiotic process of knowledge

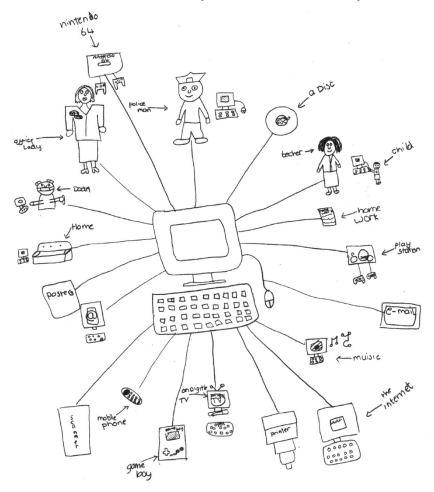

Figure 5.4 'Computers in my world' (Kelly).

construction. Knowing is formed and shaped by socially shared ways of representing. The ready-to-hand semiotic resources embedded in our everyday lives are not a neutral conduit for pre-existing concepts. By enabling certain meanings, they are formative of how we know and understand. This challenges the notion of a separation between mind and representation.

'Nothing is really being 're-presented' here; there is no separate entity, no pure mental idea, apart from the meanings made with the specific material systems of semiotic resources our culture provides us with' (Lemke, 1998: 110–111).

'JUST' SHORTHAND

Concept map nodes are generally word-based (Novak and Gowin, 1984: 176–177; Stow, 1997), although hyperlinked image is becoming increasingly common in digital mapping (e.g. Novak and Cañas, 2006). What was innovative about the 'Computers in my world' task was that, deriving from the European *Représentation* project (Crawford et al., 2003), drawing was specified as the primary mode of communication. Image takes up the larger share of graphic space. This proved to be successful because of the suitability of drawing for representing objects, people, activities and places. Sometimes children gave careful attention to detail, while on other occasions they drew a bare outline. Why should this be?

It is not necessary to represent the entirety of what is known in text making. Decisions are reached regarding what it is that is to be signified. The features picked out for representation are those characteristics deemed 'criterial' (Kress, 1997: 10–12) at a particular moment in time for defining a thing, person, event or idea in accordance with a particular purpose and in order to inform the person for whom the text is intended. 'Criteriality' is not fixed. It shifts according to what is focused on. This accounts for constancies and variations in the texts children make. Oliver populated his map exclusively with digital equipment (Figure 5.3). In contrast, Amelia's interest was in the people who use computers and what they do with them (Figure 5.6). What children choose to represent does not exclude their knowing about other aspects of phenomena. The class teacher reported that there were individuals 'who I knew could have included more information but didn't'. In subsequent interviews, the children provided additional information and explanations, spoke about their experiences, described technical issues, and so on. Made on a different day, certain constancies and differences would be anticipated—as would be the case with interviewing or a written account.

With eagerness to cooperate, the map makers endeavoured make their drawings as transparent as possible so that they would be readily comprehensible. The detail of drawings of digital games, for example, was described as 'like the clearest things that you see on them.' Decisions were made about what might and might not be of interest, what would be foregrounded, what should be withheld. With a concern for the appropriate handling of social relationships, establishing common ground entails taking into account the needs of the imagined 'readership'. Certain things can be taken for granted, and others cannot. The map makers could not assume that what was well known to them as a generation immersed in the contemporary game-playing culture of the young was known at all by the unfamiliar adult research team:

'I was looking for the most popular game thing there which probably everybody that's gone through town has seen it in the shop window.'

Texts represent children's semiotic settling at a particular moment in time. They are at the same time meaning rich and partial.

Notwithstanding disparities between texts made by different children and variations in those made by the same child, even within the same text items are not always drawn in the same way. Why is this? In her drawing of the central keyboard, Amy was exhaustive in representing each letter and number of the English numeric and alphabetic systems, which she arranged in a sequential order and as separate blocks. On the square outline shape of other keys, she inscribed symbols: four arrow keys conjoined as a group at the bottom centre along with two keys bearing punctuation marks (a 'lesser than' symbol and a full stop). Amy specifically labelled the enter key with its inverted 'L' shape, and positioned it centrally in its own space. A grid-like keyboard in her drawing of a laptop (top left) is a reduction in detail from the 43 specified characters of the central node. Is this a consequence of a loss of interest? There was no need to repeat what had already been given. Now known, the 'new' (Halliday, 1989: 55; Kress and Van Leeuwen, 2006: 179–185) of the laptop node is another digital function: from the image of the desktop screen (Amy later explained, 'Because if you go on the encyclopaedia (.) especially the one in school (.) it does come up with a world') to writing-like squiggles. She also showed that a laptop consists of a single unit that can be opened (in her use of perspective) and that it is portable (clarified in the 'hand held' label).

The rich detail of Amy's central computer contrasts sharply with the 'shorthand' of bare outline shapes devoid of attributes labelled 'computers' in the nodal cluster depicting locations (top centre). Even so, these shapes are differentiated. The vertically conjoined squares in the office may represent a laptop (Amy said, 'Some people in businesses they have laptops'—see also the adjacent node). She selected squares inside squares for the home location (one labelled 'home computer' and the other identified orally in 'I've got the Internet on my television as well'). The school computers are even less detailed (squares). What these shapes are intended to represent is contextually inferred with reference to the central node which provides the map focus. Adjustments in detail are signs of changing representational purposes. As Amy's attention was directed to the places where computers are found, her focus shifted. Distinguishing features of computers were not necessary because these are shown elsewhere. The semiotic economy of shapes is sufficient, here, to represent 'computerness'. This reduced detail enabled Amy, even within the relatively confined space and limited time available for each node, to focus on the 'new': the existence, number and positioning of computers in different locations. Drawn from a high angle as if looking down and into the doorway, her three-sided shapes provide perspective. Each of the three locations ('office', 'home' and 'Primary computer room') is drawn as a similar shape and size, although this is hardly likely to be the case in actuality. Constancy brings them together in a relationship of likeness, whilst variations differentiate them. The interiors are plan-like. Even within the confined space available, Amy shows difference. A certain perception of the world of work is depicted in the office node: the computer on a desk facing a window with a single chair, and the framed squiggly lines on the office wall, possibly representing a chart or a certificate. In selecting these features for inclusion, other items were excluded. These were the things that Amy considered, at that moment, criterial in representing an office. It suggests a very different experience from the school suite where multiple computers are arranged side by side, and repetition of like chairs is omitted. The very presence of adjustments in Amy's drawings of computers indicates attendance to different units of text in the process of design.

Design is not necessarily a case of moving sequentially from the smallest unit of representation, to relationships between parts, and then to interrelationships across the whole text. Certain decisions are made before getting started and others are made during the process of production. Scarcity of erasing across the full set of maps suggests that what the children drew first was to some extent pre-planned, and they abided by their prior and emerging structural decisions. Room for manoeuvre within the chosen structure and how that arrangement is filled becomes increasingly constrained with each successive addition. In handmade texts, presentation (e.g. size, emphasis, colour, materiality) and layout (within the frame of the graphic surface or in relation to other graphic items) are not retrospectively superimposed, but are co-produced with the detail of a drawing or choice of lexis in one graphic act. The co-presence of these resources makes even single graphic items compound in terms of layers of signifiers, and therefore multiply semiotic. As a consequence, all graphic items are actually sign complexes.

'JUST' REPETITION

Following Novak and Gowin (1984), concept maps are often analysed quantitatively (e.g. Rice, Ryan and Samson, 1998; Stoddart et al., 2000). Content analysis of the number of nodes in Chelsea's map (Figure 5.5) results in a score of nine, in comparison with 22 or 23 for Amy's (depending on whether the central node is counted as one or two items) and 26 for George's (see Mavers, Somekh and Restorick, 2002 for details of the statistical approach taken in the ImpaCT2 project). If content is further broken down into items of digital equipment, resources, places where they are used, people who use them and digitally mediated activities—respectively the 'what', 'how', 'where', 'who' and 'why' of 'Computers in my world', as specified in the task instructions (Somekh and Mavers, 2003)—this reduces Chelsea's score to just one (location of use) because she 'only' repeated the 'same' drawing. From a purely numerical perspective, this low count might suggest shortcoming. Was this inadequacy? Are amount and variation always indicators of sophistication? Did Chelsea lack the knowledge to undertake the task competently? Did she repeat images because she was short of ideas? What happens if her map is approached as serious and principled engagement with the topic?

Chelsea's map is powerful in its very repetitiousness. Repeated drawing of nine virtually identical houses is by no means deficiency. It is a way of signifying 'sameness'. Drawn with perspective from a sideways bird's-eye view, the houses are of an equal size and evenly spaced. Slight variations, for example omission of four chimneys, may have been a consequence of time constraints or the tedium of repetition—or she may have wished to imply minor disparities rather than major differences. Children frequently draw pictures that include some kind of background (e.g. Arizpe and Styles, 2003: colour plates 4, 6, 8; Millard, 2004: 151). Across the maps, objects, buildings and people are extracted from their setting. Computers are not placed on tables or desks with all the paraphernalia that normally surround them, houses are not located in a street, and so on. This is apt to a 'conceptual' rather than a 'narrative' genre (Kress and Van Leeuwen, 2006:

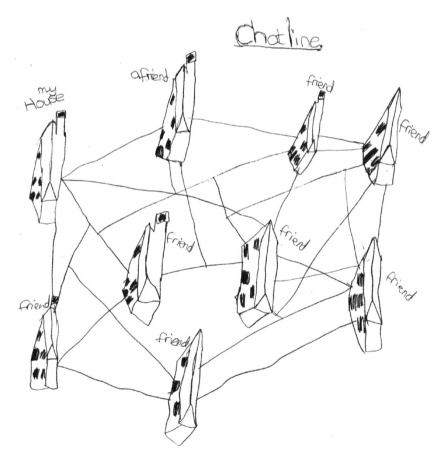

Figure 5.5 'Computers in my world' (Chelsea).

45–113) where features represent knowledge, understanding and experience of phenomena in the world, rather than the construction of character, setting and plot as pictures.

As an anchoring point, Chelsea's label 'my House' to the top extreme left assigns self-ownership and names the building. Elsewhere, repetition of drawings is matched by seven iterations of 'friend' and one of 'a friend'. This labelling does not fix what these are drawings of (i.e. she did not write 'a friend's house'). Why did she do this? In constructing a complementary relationship between image and writing, her drawings represent location and her labels name the occupants. People are not specified as individuals; they are assigned identity in relationship. This is intensified in her linkage. Each node is connected to every other by either direct or branched links (26 in total). Nodes across the full set of maps are generally linked and interlinked as in concept mapping rather than branched and 'twigged' as in mind mapping. The children sometimes explained associations which led from one idea to the next using the Buzanian term 'branched off' which, interestingly, was not mentioned in the scripted instructions. Whereas interpretation of Amelia's map (Figure 5.6) entails taking account of which line joins which drawing, and what this association might mean, Chelsea's does not demand careful tracking from one node to another. Her lines link like with like: friends communicating with one another at home. This is substantiated in her map title where she substituted the prescribed 'Computers in my world' for 'Chatline'. It is not that she did not listen to the task instructions or that she was being uncooperative or perverse, but that she wanted to give a certain view of the topic. Her map depicts interconnected communication between a social network of friends-at-home.

Repetition is there in other maps, but it is tempered. No single node recurs, but features are drawn more than once. Amelia drew five virtually identical computers (Figure 5.6). This indicates regularity of medium, just as Chelsea depicted regularity of location. Also repeated are the bodily postures of five of the people: profile, seated and oriented towards the screens, with arms bent and hands occupied. This represents commonly occurring use of computers and absorption in screen-based activities. Other repetitions show numerosity: two notes and three coins as a metaphor for wealth, 12 windows in the 'MANSHON' (mansion) and four in-line wheels on the limousine to represent opulence, 31 square keys on the keyboard, plus seven small shaded circles and three unshaded squares on the monitor and processing unit to show operational regularity.

In contrast, no word is repeated. Labelling was prescribed, but how to label was not specified. This gave choice. In a sideways orientation, the screen displays cannot be seen on the almost identical drawings of computers-in-use, so the map 'reader' is not privy to the specifics of what the represented people are doing. This must be obtained from the labels. The nouns, 'GAMES', 'BUSINESS' and 'E-MAIL' written in capital letters name respectively leisure-based content-rich activities, domain and a content-free means of communication, but she did not draw them. This also applies to her representations of homework and schoolwork to the right of her map, where the activity is linked as a separate node rather than as a label. Drawing takes on other semiotic functionalities: Amelia characterized the identities, attitudes and actions associated with these pursuits. Identity is not named, but shown. People dress differently when they use computers for different purposes: a peaked cap for game playing and a formal striped shirt for work, whilst clothing is unspecified in the email node. Gender is suggested in the length and style of hair. Attitudes and the affective are represented in facial expression. The neutral line of the bespectacled businessman's mouth (centre left) endows him with a seriousness that contrasts with the achievement and enjoyment depicted in the wide smiles of the email messagers and the game player (the latter intensified in the linked node where frontal orientation shows the facial expression of a broad smile and closed eyes, along with the actional stance of raised arms and clenched fists). In specifying how different digitally mediated activities are operated, arms are extended and hands are occupied with typing (made absolutely explicit through raised keys), grasping the joystick and operating the mouse. The individuality of game-playing, business and email messaging contrasts with collaborative use of the computer in school, shown as two back-facing girls, one pointing upwards at

Figure 5.6   'Computers in my world' (Amelia).

the screen and the other with arm outstretched towards, and presumably operating, the keyboard. Amelia's map shows that computers can be used by different people for different purposes. Interplays between drawing and labelling expand meaning potentiality, and Amelia made them work together in a co-construction of meaning. No one component is dispensable in the semiotic plenitude of her design.

Elsewhere, it might appear that drawing and labelling are repetitions of one another. Take, for example, the items of equipment in Oliver's map (Figure 5.3). Image and writing share the function of identification. It might be argued that one mode could substitute the other. His map would remain meaningful if either the drawings or the labels were to be removed. Does this make one or the other redundant? Does one replicate the other? It is because these are such familiar items that naming and showing are apparently obvious. However, congruity is not the same as replication. The 'anchorage' (Barthes, 1977: 38–41) of labelling reduces the risk of misconstrual. Amelia's building to the top centre of her map is fixed as a library rather than a house, a school or a hotel. Her label 'MANSHON' (mansion) indicates a class of object, whilst her drawing shows affluence in architecture that departs from ordinariness (a domed roof and pointed towers unlike Chelsea's more typical English houses), an external feature that signifies the exotic (a fountain or palm tree) and wealth represented in the stretched limousine. Openness is constrained. With more special-ized knowledge of types of equipment such as a range of popular digital games technologies, Oliver's labels and specification of attributes provide details that might not be familiar to less-knowledgeable 'readers'. An adult researcher may not know what these devices are called or what they look like. Drawn and written identification are not a repetition of one another. Each supplies different kinds of facts: what something looks like and what it is called. This is a mutually inter-reliant semiotic relationship. Together, the drawing and the label co-fix meaning.

DISCUSSION

Closer examination of 'jumble', shorthand and repetition discourages, even dispels, over hasty verdicts of 'messiness', cutting corners or lack of effort. What at first sight may appear to be inadequacy might turn out to be sophistication. Meanings are layered. They reside in signs and sign com-plexes, and in semiotic interdependency between signs and sign complexes in the interweaving of *textus*. Semiotic interplays expand meaning poten-tiality. Meanings in one graphic feature illuminate meanings elsewhere. The countless ways in which signs can be made and combined provide the potential for infinite design possibilities. Here, drawing, labelling, layout and linkage in a diagrammatic structure provided the means for organizing examples of and constructing relationships between items of technological equipment, who uses them, how, why and where. Each choice is significant, and the outcome is a complex ensemble. Children represent meanings effectively, economically, skilfully and succinctly in a variety of ways. If the unremarkable in understated semiotic orchestrations is taken seriously, the complexity and intricacy of texts made by even relatively young children become remarkable.

Just as features beyond the language of speech such as tone, rhythm, intonation and volume are commonly designated prosodics (or suprasegmental), punctuation, underlining and 'other forms of emphasis' are generally thought of as 'paragraphalogical' or the 'co-text' (Halliday, 1978: 133). With this terminology, the prefixes 'para' and 'co' subordinate features of writing beyond lexis and syntax to a supplementary, even subsidiary, function. Extended to graphic multimodality, lines-as-links, encircling and scale might be similarly subordinated. Yet layout provides ways of making meaning beyond lexis and the subject matter of drawing. Presentation, arrangement and linkage can be made to carry meanings that drawings and language do not. Subjugation of these graphic features to an ancillary role is unsustainable in an approach which insists that all features of text warrant serious attention.

Through their interpretation and making of signs for a variety of purposes and in different social environments, children experience, engage with, figure out, analyse, evaluate and reflect on how meanings are made. For example, how children draw entirely ordinary things—noses, trees, containers—derives from the culture, heritage, place, time, socio-economy and educational practices in which they participate (Court, 1992; Paget, 1932; Wilson and Ligtvoet, 1992). The material presence of a graphic feature is a trace of a signifying resource available at that time to the text maker. What can be deduced from texts produced over time are the semiotic reservoirs available to individuals. It can be inferred that, from the range of resources available to them, children select what is needed in order to make particular meanings. Conversely, absence of a feature does not necessarily mean that it was not available, but that it was not selected for whatever reason. Choice is subject to what is available. As a consequence of different semiotic histories, the design options available to individuals vary. Opportunities to investigate with children how they have made meaning, and to share the range of ways in which meanings can be made in the particular genre—here the drawing, labelling, relative size, framing, arrangement and links possible in the diagrammatic structure of mapping—can be one means of expanding semiotic reservoirs.

6   Fleeting Texts

Children's drawing and writing have varying degrees of permanence. Durability is dependent on what is valued as well as the affordances of media and the practices associated with them. From the multitude of texts children produce, some are kept, some are discarded, and some are forgotten or lost. Parents save those they prize, and schools retain curricular work for the purposes of assessment and accountability. Other texts have a fleeting existence: those made with a stick in the sand, fingers in condensation on a window or chalk on tarmac. Unless these are recorded, they are short-lived, ephemeral, here and gone in a moment. Does transience equate with worthlessness? Does temporariness preclude or dilute semiotic work?

THE FRAMING OF MEDIUM

As physical beings, we engage with the world and with one another through our bodies and with the material resources available to us. Each of our senses provides us with particular kinds of information which we combine in complex ways to make meaning (Finnegan, 2002). Drawing and writing cannot exist apart from their materiality. A characteristic shared with other humanly fashioned objects such as buildings, furniture, toys and clothing is a material existence as a semi-permanent 'thing' that occupies space. Graphic matter is visual—and writing is as much visual as drawing, whether the exquisite calligraphy of illuminated manuscripts or a scribbled list on the back of a used envelope. Like all humanly crafted objects, graphic artefacts are also tangible; the weight and texture of paper are experienced in their tactility, as are certain inscriptional substances and indentations on the page. Tissue paper scrunches, crinkles and rustles, whilst laminated card is difficult to bend and shiny finishes squeak when rubbed. Surfaces can also carry different scents either intrinsic to themselves (e.g. a new book or freshly opened ream of paper), or brought about by storage (e.g. a musty smell suggests age or damp). Less often, aroma can be deliberately applied, such as smearing with blackcurrant scented rollerblade wax (Ormerod and Ivanic, 2002: 69).

Handmade texts are always produced materially, and that materiality is always meaningful. Natural and humanly crafted or manufactured properties offer certain semiotic possibilities and constraints, and these are factored into the design process. The material attributes of surface, substance and tool shape what can and cannot be done. Their combined material properties coalesce with regard to representational affordance, determining, shaping, suggesting or leaving entirely open what might or might not be done. Compare, for example, ballpoint pen, different breadths of felt tips, wax crayons, sharpened or blunt coloured pencils, charcoal or pastels on paper or card of different colours, textures, finishes, qualities and sizes. Hues vary depending on whether they are applied to a white or coloured surface. Ink blots spread on roughly textured paper, and pool on a shiny surface. Choice of medium affects what can be done, and one choice is dependent on, or has implications for, another.

Children's choice of surface, substance and tool for their drawing and writing—or that made for them—is not arbitrary. Resolutions are made about the most apt medium for the particular purpose from what is available. There is semiotic significance in which media are settled upon, and how those material resources are used. Gold leaf of the richest quality applied 'lavishly' and imported lapis lazuli (Oakeshott, 1981: 3) signified the wealth and power of those who commissioned the Winchester Bible in Medieval England. In contemporary society, it is not that everyday substances such as pencil or ballpoint pen are meaningless, but that they signify the ordinary. Even so, as representational practices shift with the social context, ordinariness is not fixed. Ballpoint pen might be commonplace at home, but in younger primary classrooms, it becomes the tool of the teacher and not of the child. Choice of medium is dependent on purpose, and purpose is always socially and 'ideationally' (Halliday, 1978: 112) specific. It follows that which medium is selected is inextricably bound up with why the text is being made and for whom, as well as the environment in which it is produced. Overlooking the materiality of children's drawn and written texts is to disregard an essential feature of what they are, and is neglectful of their semiotic plenitude.

Use of medium is socially regulated. Practices may or may not be shared between social environments, and this frames design possibilities. What is feasible is subject to what is available or what can be acquired, as well as rules around acceptable use—and this shifts from context to context. At home, certain ordinary, everyday resources are supplied, to hand or readily accessible, whilst others must be obtained with permission. Children take initiative as they seek out and gather resources before getting started, and disappear to find things as they are needed. Amongst my collection of texts made by children at home, surfaces include the reverse of an out-of-date calendar, the cover of a small red notebook, tractor-feed printing paper, coloured card, a decorative frame cut from a magazine; substances include pencil, ballpoint pen, felt tip, wax crayon and paint; and affixed materials include glitter, foil, card, items cut from greetings cards and magazines, wool, lace and ribbon. Tightly regulated, there are fairly strict rules around what can and cannot be used and when in the classroom. Certain ordinary, everyday resources are supplied and readily accessible, whilst others are restricted to certain activities. To hand for ongoing use, in the centre of each table in one school were, variously, exercise books, pencils, black fibre tip pens, coloured felt tip pens, coloured pencils, erasers, non-permanent markers, rulers, glue sticks and scissors. Children reached, deliberated, shared, seized and sought from elsewhere.

Individual dry-wipe whiteboards have become popular in primary schools in England over recent years. Non-permanent pen on a shiny plasticized surface is intended to be provisional; these boards are regularly used and reused. This is not a new phenomenon. Chalk on slate could be rubbed off and wax tablets scored with a stylus were intended to be smoothed over (Clanchy, 1993: 118–119; Ong, 1982: 94). Fixed momentarily and erased without trace soon after, these texts have a fleeting existence. This undoes the commonly held view that graphic text is permanent. Like much of what goes on in the pedagogic exchange of the classroom, whiteboard texts are lost as a permanent record, but are pivotal to the dynamism of the 'episode' within the course of the lesson. As 'points of fixing' in the 'semiotic chain' (Stein, 2008: 113) of learning, they punctuate the ongoing semiotic flow of activities and interactions. Even if transient—here and gone in a moment—these punctuations represent a semiotic settling at this moment in time. As streams of semiosis precede and succeed the production of text, meaning making is not fixed and may be revised or supplemented later—either immediately or soon afterwards, or even many months or years hence.

Specification of medium is one way of shaping text making. Provision of a broad, round-ended marker and an A4 board exacts scale. In conjunction with the practice of display and limited time for completion, this combination of tool and surface limits the amount of writing and the detail of drawing possible; it compels representational thrift. Due to the graphic space available, texts must be brief and succinct. What could be described at length must be condensed, and at the same time remain sufficient to need. At a cursory glance the hypotheses predicting the outcome of an investigation into magnetic force produced on individual dry-wipe whiteboards by a class of 7- and 8-year-olds might appear to be 'just' a few quick drawings consisting of uncomplicated shapes, lines and shading, some without any writing at all, with an average of 5.8 words per board across the class set (Figure 6.1). Brevity might be judged as deficiency. Examined with a different lens, something short and produced quickly, even over a few moments, can be seen as demanding of semiotic work. Even when texts are short-lived, children are discriminating in their shaping of meaning.

RESPONDING TO THE FRAMING OF ESTABLISHED CLASSROOM PRACTICES

Due to time constraints and suitable pacing to retain student attention, it would be impractical for each child in the class to articulate their response to teacher questioning one by one. A practice that has become established in English schools over recent years is the individual production and display of texts in the context of whole-class teaching. In response to quick-fire, in-the-moment, teacher-framed tasks, students write and sometimes draw with non-permanent fibre tip pens on small dry-wipe whiteboards (e.g. spelling patterns or mathematical problems). As a graphic substitute for a face-to-face response, a pedagogic benefit of this medium is that everyone can contribute, and at the same time. The spatial simultaneity of holding up dry-wipe whiteboard texts across the public space of the classroom allows for scanning of responses across the whole class. These overviews enable teachers to monitor students' engagement, to assess existing and developing knowledge, skills and understanding, and to make judgements regarding the achievements and the needs of the class as a whole and of individuals within it, informing how to proceed in supporting the 'where next' of learning. For the class, it provides possibilities for peer assessment, self-comparison and learning from others.

Display on individual dry-wipe whiteboards presupposes an 'audience' of 'viewers'. Semiotically, this marks a shift from representation to communication. From moment to moment the flow of social interaction carves out boundaries with regard to what is and is not relevant, and this has implications for keeping up. The design of drawing and writing for the

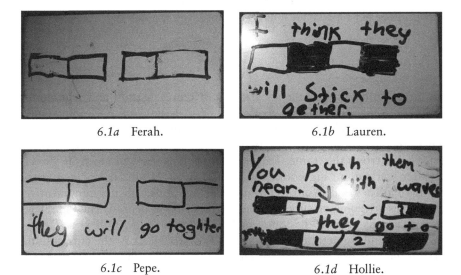

6.1a   Ferah.   6.1b   Lauren.

6.1c   Pepe.   6.1d   Hollie.

Figure 6.1   Dry-wipe whiteboard hypotheses.

purpose of display in the interactional exchange of the classroom demands consideration of coherence with the unfolding of the lesson in terms of what needs to be inscribed at this moment and what can go unrepresented. Judgements are made about what is known and what needs to be known. A context of shared experience allows the text maker to formulate certain assumptions. Ferah's whiteboard text consists of image only (Figure 6.1a). Isolated from the lesson, this might be interpreted as a drawing of railings, a mathematical solution to dividing shapes into two equal halves, or a host of other things. Located in the context of the activity in and for which her text was produced, what her two drawings represented could be taken for granted without the 'anchorage' (Barthes, 1977: 39–40) of a written label because everyone in the class shared the collective known that, in this lesson, divided rectangles denoted bar magnets.

As the display of dry-wipe whiteboard texts is a familiar everyday practice in many contemporary schools, children are well aware of the possibility that what is inscribed privately—or semi-privately—may be subject to public scrutiny, and that they might be asked to describe, clarify, explain or justify. In this lesson, seven whiteboards selected by the teacher for particular focus over a period of 1 minute 44 seconds of whole-class exchange entailed showing and questioning / response. Where her drawing-only text was seemingly 'just' a re-presentation of the bar magnets that remained positioned apart on the class screen, Ferah was able to supplement her graphic hypothesis with the spoken explanation that 'they're going to stay where they are.' Supplying additional information in face-to-face exchange removed the need for the kind of explicitness that would be required in more permanent texts and, in addition to the affordances of a medium suited to display (i.e. a scale sufficient to be seen clearly from a distance), accounts for her representational economy.

PEDAGOGIC FRAMING

Children manage simultaneous streams of representation and communication as a matter of course. For example, it is not unusual for playing, eating, watching television, participating in family interaction, monitoring what others are doing and more besides to go on concurrently. Whole-class teaching narrows the frame. Teachers marshal a variety of means to direct children's attention: big books, puppets, dramatization, artefacts, and so on. Even as they endeavour to minimize distractions, other communicative exchanges are going on simultaneously. These might be transient and relate to interactions around the topic, such as a joking aside. Others are more sustained, and, sometimes disconnected from the work of the curriculum, may at the time be considered (by children, but not by the teacher) pressing issues, such as a purse and an oral message being illicitly passed between a group and covert compilation of a list of email addresses. Entirely ordinary,

Table 6.1 Framing the Task (28 seconds)

	Gesture		Speech
a)		places the bar magnets on the visualiser	*okay (.)*
b)		touches each bar magnet and adjusts them slightly	*two bar magnets (..)*
c)			*now looking back to what our aim for today was (.) Tom (..) okay (..) we will learn that forces act between two magnets (..)*
d)		touches each bar magnet and adjusts them slightly	*so there are our two magnets* *okay (..)*
e)			*what do you think (.) think about this (.) don't put your hands up for now (.)*
f)		touches each bar magnet and adjusts them slightly	*if I (..) move them*
g)		brings fingers together above the magnets	*closer together (..)*
h)			*then let go (..) what do you think would happen to the magnets?*

in the classroom children decide where to direct their attention in the dynamic unfolding of lessons.

Scale is one means of commanding attention. Using a visualiser—a digital display technology consisting of a high quality video camera connected to a data projector—the teacher presented two bar magnets to the class. Their differently coloured ends could be seen but were not mentioned, and neither was their horizontal orientation (Table 6.1). Placement established visually and without spoken explanation the experimental conditions that would be required in subsequent hands-on investigation. Entirely ordinary yet surprising in its complexity and pace, the teacher simulated the experimental method of moving the magnets 'closer together' in a multimodal ensemble of action and gesture synchronized with speech (Table 6.1f–g), and invited the prediction of what would happen next (Table 6.1h). Here and gone, the sounds of speech and the spatio-temporality of gesture were momentary. One glance away at this critical moment, or an aural distraction, and an essential feature of the task framing might be missed.

Primary education is typified by a range of diverse teaching and learning activities. In the pedagogic exchange of whole-class interaction, communication around curricular entities happens in fast-changing, if entirely ordinary, modal shifts and multimodal ensembles (e.g. combinations of speech, gesture, writing), and across sites of display (e.g. the body, the screen, the page). The science classroom is complexly constructed representationally (Kress et al., 2001; Lemke, 2000). Prior to his instructions with regard to hypothesizing, the teacher read out from the class screen, showed and named magnets, asked questions, explained, enacted processes, elicited scientific terminology and made a mind map. As signs accrue, children constantly make decisions about what to attend to and when in the unrelenting and entirely ordinary semiotic flow of the lesson. This has consequences later on, when from the immense diversity of what has gone on, tasks are set that require the extraction of key features from the semiotic accumulation of what has gone on previously.

RESPONDING TO PRIOR FRAMING

Pedagogy is not delivery and acquisition, but communication. The semiotic work of the classroom entails interpreting of what is seen, heard and done, and responding in ways that are apt. Aptness requires the design of a response that fits. Tracking back from children's text making to its prior—and often transitory—pedagogic origins, the complexity of what is commonly taken to be straightforward is striking. From the framing of digitally mediated face-to-face interaction—choice and positioning of objects, actions on them and gestures around them displayed on the class screen with simultaneous speech—the children were required to respond in drawing and writing.

Redesigning with graphic representational resources subject matter originating in the multimodal interactions of embodied exchange entails certain representational shifts. How did the class handle this?

In compliance with their teacher's instructions 'You're going to take a whiteboard and a whiteboard pen and draw the two magnets', everyone in the class drew. Without exception, all 27 children re-presented the bar magnets as freehand rectangular shapes (Figure 6.1). Constancy of visual resemblance was further established by dividing the oblong with a centrally positioned vertical line (e.g. Figure 6.1a, c). Seen on the class screen but not yet mentioned by the teacher, the decision had to be made as to whether the different colour of each of the two ends was significant. Nineteen students (70%) added shading (e.g. Figure 6.1b, d). Restricted to black marker, the red and blue ends of the magnets-as-objects could be differentiated but not specified. In order to supply this detail, four students in the class added colour labels (either the whole words or their initial letters). Also unanimous across the class, alignment of the rectangles in a horizontal orientation and on the same plane was a re-presentation of the teacher's arrangement displayed on the class screen. No one drew them vertically, at an angle or offset. Layout was assumed to be significant for the experiment, and perhaps implied visually by the teacher's touching and slight adjustment (Table 6.1b, d, f). The children's drawings can be traced back to their interpretations of what they saw. Deriving from what had been given, they made judgements regarding what they considered criterial to the immediate objective. This is not a free flow of meaning, nor is it a matter of unproblematic 'translation'. What is produced is a fresh semiotic entity. Knowledge and identity are constructed when signs made with the resources of different modes and media are newly made and elaborated in a process of reconfiguration and recontextualization (Selander, 2008).

Demonstrating engagement with pedagogic tasks entails factoring in existing knowledge. Predominance of attraction (81% of the texts) as the anticipated outcome of the investigation was an entirely reasonable deduction based on the experiences that the children brought to the classroom with them. Lauren talked about constructing her name on her fridge door with multicoloured magnetic letters. Hollie described a magnetic fishing game:

> 'There's like this game sometimes what you get out of comics (..) like you have this pretend board (..) and there's magnetics on a board and a magnetic on a fish map (.) and you have to try and catch it.'

Others talked about 'doing magnets' earlier on in their schooling, when the curriculum specifies that students should be taught to sort objects on the basis of their material properties, one example being whether they are magnetic or non-magnetic (DfEE and QCA, 1999: 80). Amira reflected:

'I've been to two schools before and I learnt about magnets in there (..) well I haven't learnt about forces and that (..) but I did learn about how they stick and all the other different kinds of magnets.'

Experiences of objects across sites and social environments are charac-terized by constancy and diversity in what items are (e.g. small magnets attached to components of a fishing game as against a box of identical bar magnets available for scientific investigation) and in how they are used (e.g. a child-initiated game played at home as against a teacher-directed experi-ment conducted in the classroom). These different frames shape similari-ties and variations in what is done, which features are made salient and the interactions that go on around them. In a similar way, literacy 'events' are differentially constructed and understood according to the particular social, economic and cultural community, with consequences for diver-sity between, not deficiency in, children's home and school experience of reading (Heath, 1983). As phenomena are approached, handled and inter-preted in different ways in different social environments, this shapes what is engaged with and what is learned.

'Recontextualising the concept in new domains allows it to migrate from familiar domains and attach itself to a new conceptual territory, which in turn produces new variations on the concept and subsequently new texts' (Stein, 2008: 118).

Experiences in different social environments can consolidate, extend and deepen, as well as confuse and challenge.

THE FRAMING OF MODE

A precise interpretation of the instruction to 'show me what you think is going to happen to these two magnets', 23 students (85% of the class) selected drawing to represent the predicted outcome of the forthcoming investigation, and the only way in the nine image-only texts. Alteration of positioning from the experimental conditions of apartness that remained displayed on the class screen (Table 6.1h) to the conjoined shapes of the whiteboard drawing indicated that attraction should be inferred as the hypothesized outcome of the forthcoming investigation. Drawn as one oblong divided by vertical lines, Amira later explained, 'I like drawed like three or four little lines in the bar magnet to make it look like two of them are stuck together.' In hypothesizing the outcome of a forthcoming inves-tigation, dry-wipe whiteboards provided a transitory meaning space where it was acceptable for scientific correctness not to be entirely settled. This legitimized 'having a go'. There was a correspondence between the provi-sionality of the medium and the provisionality of hypothesizing.

The co-presence of drawing and writing puts them into a relationship where the multimodal ensemble provides scope for designing intermodal relations of meaning. Sixteen members of the class (59%) chose to write an explanation after they had drawn. How did the children deploy the resources of these modes and how did they distribute meaning? Lauren drew two conjoined magnets and then wrote 'I think they will stick to gether (together)' (Figure 6.1b). In a relationship of meaning congruence (see also Chapter 5), the 'ideational' (Halliday, 1978: 112) notion of attraction is shared. However, writing is not a replication of image. Lauren's drawing shows the matched shape, equal size and differently coloured ends of the bar magnets, and also the anticipated post-experimental spatial relationships in joined positioning and horizontal orientation. In Pepe's text, the meanings made in drawing and writing are complementary (Figure 6.1c). His image shows the magnets in their separated pre-experimental positions, whilst his writing—'they will go toghter (together)'—hypothesizes what will happen. Drawing on Halliday and Hasan (e.g. 1976), this intermodal relationship might be described as an 'expectancy relation' (Royce, 2002: 194).

Linguistic cohesion refers to relations of meaning (Halliday and Hasan, 1976: 1–30). In an anaphoric relationship, reference is made back to something that has been given earlier (ibid.: 2). For example, in 'Like poles repel. Try pushing them together.' the pronoun 'them' refers back to the adjectivally defined plural noun 'like poles'. Across the class set of 27 whiteboard texts, only two name the magnets. Of those that incorporate a written explanation, 75% include the pronouns 'it' or 'they' and exclude the noun (e.g. Figure 6.1b, c, d). Cohesion is created multimodally in a mutually dependent relationship between drawing and written words. Pronouns subsist in relation to the specification of image, and drawings identify the subject of written explanations. In a bond of multimodal interconnection rather than linguistic cohesion, one mode is relationally dependent on another.

What are signs of learning? Where do we look for them? Retained for the purposes of tracking attainment over time and for accountability purposes, it is largely graphic texts rather than the dynamic interactions that take place around them, including embodied representation such as enactment or giving a demonstration, that ultimately count. Looking beyond their drawing and writing, can children demonstrate their learning by other means? Professional judgements do include observations. Teachers do respond to the variety of ways in which learning is demonstrated as a matter or course, but immersed in the work of the everyday classroom, they cannot be everywhere at once. If learning happens multimodally across a range of activities but assessment focuses primarily on language, much of what children have learned might potentially be overlooked. Given opportunities to attend to how children make meaning in a variety of ways, educators might be better positioned to understand and support their learning.

Embodied texts in the classroom are here and gone. In simultaneous speech and gesture-as-enactment, Hollie rehearsed for the rest of the class an exchange she had engaged in with Yadin during paired debate. Clenching her fists to represent bar magnets, she positioned them in a horizontally parallel orientation and moved them slightly inwards towards one another, as she said, 'When you have two magnets at the same time and when you push them together' (Table 6.2b–d). Uncurling her fingers so that her hands remained at a distance and on a matched horizontal plane, her open palms now faced one another. She made two slight converging punches on each occurrence of 'harder' as she continued, 'they get harder and harder' (Table 6.2e) and then snapped her palms together on the 'get' of 'to get together' (Table 6.2f).

As, in the classroom, children move between different modes and multimodal ensembles of representation, often stipulated by the teacher, certain resources become available. In engaging with the curricular entity of magnetic force, some aspects of the phenomenon were realized across modes, whilst others were modally particular (Table 6.3). Continuity of meaning was realized with different resources. Numerosity was cross-modally defined: in speech ('one', 'two', 'each') and in paired drawings and fists. The

Table 6.2   Reporting to the Class (Hollie)

	Speech	Gesture	
a)	*I was saying to Yadin*		
b)	*when you have two magnets*		clasps and raises fists apart as if lifting objects
c)	*at the same time*		tightens fists
d)	*and you push them together*		moves fists slightly inwards
e)	*they get harder and harder*		brings flat palms together as if with effort
f)	*to get together*		snaps open palms together

movement of attraction was enacted, was drawn in the dry-wipe whiteboard hypothesis by four children as wavy lines to represent magnetic waves, was described in the words 'push' and 'stick' and later the term 'attract', and, in a subsequent worksheet, as arrows (see Chapter 4). Directionality was shown gesturally (e.g. moving hands together) and lexically (e.g. 'together'), as well as with arrowheads. Even so, there was not necessarily equivalence of meaning. Hollie represented the outcome of attraction as conjoining in gesture (palms together), in drawing (joined ends) and in speech (e.g. 'together'), but the precise point of joining was shown only in spatial modes, namely as corresponding positioning of hands in gesture and a common line in drawing. Certain meanings were modally exclusive. Shape, identical size, horizontal alignment and plane were shown in drawing and clenched fists, but were absent from speech and writing. Bar magnets were named early on, whereas poles were initially represented as dividing lines and shading, were technically termed later on and were absent in enactment. Hollie articulated the speed of attraction as 'harder and harder', and enacted it as arduous punches followed by a sudden and rapid pull with the 'snapping' together of palms, but pace was not articulated in speech or represented in writing, and was absent from arrows. Combining the spatial modes of drawing and writing, and the temporal mode of speech with the spatio-temporal mode of gesture, enabled the children to distribute meaning multimodally. Together, this provided the means to both intensify and disperse meanings. Each fresh realization entailed reconfigurations of form and meaning. It is not that one

Table 6.3 Modal Distribution of Meaning (Hollie)

	Lexis	Enactment	Drawing
Naming	bar magnets		
Enumerating	one, two, each	hands	pairing
Shape		fists	rectangles
Size		fists	rectangles
Properties	north / south poles, ends		vertical dividing line, shading
Position	apart, together	apart, touching	apart, conjoined
Alignment		horizontally	horizontality
Plane		arrangement	arrangement
Movement	go, push, attract	speed	arrows, wavy lines
Directionality	towards	inwards, outwards	arrows

mode is 'better' or 'worse' than another, but that different modes enable attendance to particular aspects of meaning.

Meaning making is fluid and dynamic as it moves across modes and through time and space. Across the 'semiotic chain' (Stein, 2008: 98) of a curricular topic, texts are realized in diverse modal configurations and multimodal ensembles. In 'endless cycles of variations' (ibid.: 119) on the theme of character in students' representations across drawing, writing, drama and three-dimensional models, 'multiple variations on a concept' (ibid.: 118) were made possible. As they move from one mode to another and construct a variety of multimodal ensembles, different resources become available, and this enables 'migration' into 'new conceptual territory' (ibid.: 118). Understanding constancies and shifts in what can be represented across modes is significant for the design of learning activities and for enabling children to demonstrate their knowledge.

Flow of meaning across the semiotic chain of a curricular topic moves across modes and media, reaches backwards and forwards over time and is socially distributed in interactional exchange with others. In an ongoing stream of semiosis, text making fixes meaning more or less permanently as a material entity. It is a semiotic settling on what is deemed suitable here and now. What is represented at another time may be alike or different in more or less substantive ways. The metaphor of chaining is useful for interactional sequences around a topic where one instantiation is linked temporally to what comes immediately before and after. Just as writing and drawing are produced temporally but exist spatially, semiosis happens temporally and results in a web, rather than a chain, of linked and interlinked meanings.

THE FRAMING OF THE CURRICULAR SUBJECT

The page may be graphically blank, but designs are already generically and discursively pre-shaped by the practices of the semiotic domain in which text making is located and for which it is intended. Being a good primary school scientist includes making texts in ways that are apt (DfEE and QCA, 1999: 83). With regard to language, this includes the use of specialized terminology in procedural, observational and explanatory genres (Unsworth, 2001: 113–147). As they combine writing, calculations, diagrams, charts and graphs, recording in the science classroom demands that students make choices within and between the modes of writing and drawing in response to the framing of the task, and that they select and combine resources in ways that are acceptable to the conventional practices of this curricular subject.

Notwithstanding the ephemerality of the dry-wipe whiteboard texts and the limited time allocated to complete the hypothesis (2 minutes 38 seconds), the class recorded in ways apt to the science curriculum. In English schools, being a school scientist requires systematic investigative skills such as planning experiments, making predictions, undertaking systematic observation, presenting evidence and explaining outcomes (DfEE and QCA, 1999: 83–84). Hollie's production was modally segmented: first she drew, then she wrote, next she labelled and finally she shaded. The top half of her whiteboard text consists of methodological and theoretical information. Procedural, her upper image shows the prior experimental conditions of separation and her writing describes method: the empirical work of the scientist. (Note her substitution of the 'I' of her teacher's earlier spoken words 'if I move them closer together' (Table 6.1f-g) with the impersonality of 'You' rather than 'He', as apt to the natural sciences.) Hollie added two matched pairs of short, parallel wavy lines between her upper drawings. Undulating marks depicting curling smoke (Cox, 1992: 86) and ripples of water (ibid.: 66) are a re-production of what can be seen. Their common use for the Peircian 'indexicality' (Buchler, 1955: 108–109) of smell or heat—and here magnetic force—is metaphorical. In contrast with the speedy and uninterrupted continuousness of her drawing, some faltering prior to her inscription of 'With waves' seems to mark a moment of hesitation as she searched for terminology not provided either before or subsequently in the lesson by her teacher. Hollie later explained, 'On my one I put the magnetic waves […] I put them (*i.e. the drawings of bar magnets*) like that far apart that the magnetic waves will pull it.' Using 'appropriate scientific language and terms […] to communicate ideas and explain the behaviour of living things, materials, phenomena and processes' (DfEE and QCA, 1999: 89) is highly valued educationally. (Note also her exchange of 'move' with 'push' which may derive from the earlier mind map.)

Hollie's lower drawing predicts the outcome of the investigation. Tense is not a resource of image. Repetition of a pair of divided rectangles arranged one above the other represents present and predicted future as a change in space at a later moment in time. (Note how she shaded and labelled with numbers in order to make explicit that these are not four co-present identical objects, but the same two in different positions.) So why did Hollie opt for the present rather than the future tense in 'they go to-gether', as would befit a hypothesis? The force of attraction was something she had experienced previously:

'At home I had this magnetic doll from Groovy Girls (.) and you can dress it up (..) do you know when you've got loads of stuff that you want to put on it's hard to push it off (.) 'cos there's only allowed a certain amount of magnetics on (..) there's one big magnetic which has the person (.) then you just have to stick clothes on and all that on (..) so that's hard.'

Together, her choice of the present tense and her conjoining of the two rectangles constitute her generalization of a scientific 'truth'.

DISCUSSION

The children's predictions were both retrospective in terms of their pedagogic and personal origins, and prospective with regard to anticipated
future experimental outcomes. Tracking back from children's drawing and
writing to some of their communicational and representational origins in
the lesson —and factoring in semiotic pathways that reach back to the more
distant past of individual semiotic histories—as well as forward to their
anticipated trajectories of use can provide opportunities to investigate the
relationality between graphic text making and the interactional pedagogy
of the classroom. Even so, indeterminacy remains. The origins of certain
features of children's drawing and writing might be more or less traceable,
or more or less inconclusive. Seeking the provenance of children's texts is
not an attempt to bound, to reify, to close down, to provide a definitive
explanation, but rather to flag the complexities of punctuations of semiotic
flow in the complex environment of the classroom.

Providing a variety of activities is well acknowledged in good pedagogic
practice as being conducive to learning. In contemporary educational circles,
this is often accredited to the accommodation of different learning styles
(Gardner, 1984). An alternative view is that which modes are 'mobilized
to do certain things at certain times' (Iedema, 2003: 29), how, when and
why has implications for the semiotics of the classroom because it enables
children to engage with particular aspects of curricular entities. Entirely
ordinary and everyday, school-based learning entails the interpretation of
meanings made in a multiplicity of ways, and remaking these in the same
and different ways. This demands semiotic work. From the sheer volume
of constantly changing modal configurations and multimodal ensembles
and the selectivity of children's engagement on this particular occasion,
something happens. That 'something' is what, in part, constitutes learning. Each interpretation and each fresh realization of meaning is some kind
of expansion in the semiotic capacity of the individual (Kress, 2007: 24),
however slight and incremental. Inscribed in the semiotic work of engaging
with topics in different ways are opportunities to challenge, extend and
deepen knowledge and learning.

7 Remaking

The origins of children's drawing and writing may be more or less trace-able or more or less inconclusive (see Chapters 3 and 6). Even so, there are occasions when children deliberately remake one text as another. A prior design is remade, and the 'new' derives from the existing, as in copying (see Chapter 2). Where remaking entails a shift of mode (e.g. from writing to drawing) or across medium and mode (e.g. from drawing to enactment), certain semiotic work is required because the resources of the 'source' and 'destination' texts do not match. Surprisingly little is known about this. What processes are involved? What needs to be known and understood about different modes and media of representation and how they interre-late? What can and cannot be done? What happens to form? What happens to meaning?

REMAKING REPRESENTATION

The resources available in one mode are not necessarily available in another. Nouns and adjectives do not exist in drawing, intonation is not a feature of writing and continuousness of movement is not present in a still image. At the same time, size and arrangement are shared in the spa-tiality of graphic modes, speed—albeit named pace in speech and tempo in music—is unavoidable in temporal modes, and movement through space and time is a feature of the spatio-temporality of moving image and gesture. It is not that meaning is entirely modally confined. Writing and drawing both provide opportunities for identification, explanation, comparison, persuasion and argumentation. Some objects, people and places can be drawn or lexicalized as nouns (e.g. ☎ or 'telephone'), some descriptions can be realized as adjectives or drawn attributes (e.g. black or ●), and some actions can be represented in image and as verbs (e.g. ⛷ or 'skiing'). Even so, shifts in form bring with them shifts in meaning. The image of a dial telephone specifies the more generalized noun—which, as speech, would be materialized in voice with particular timbre (perhaps suggesting gender or age) and certain intonation (implying a question, surprise, disgust, insistence etc.). Choice of mode constitutes an episte-mological commitment; it enables different kinds of engagement with the world (Kress, 2003: 50). How phenomena and relations between them are represented has implications for which aspects of meaning can be represented, with consequences for different shapes to knowledge (West and Rostvall, 2003). This challenges the assumption that there can be any direct transfer between or unproblematic, straightforward 'translation' of one modal realization into another.

What to name processes depends on precisely which process is being inves-tigated. 'Transduction' refers to the agentive act of shifting semiotic material across modes (Bezemer and Kress, 2008: 175–182; Kress, 1997: 29). 'Trans-modalism' is concerned with 'travel across modes' of representation and com-munication—and this always contextralized, as when South African students' remaking of the canonical text of Shakespeare as three-dimensional masks was shaped by the historically located social, cultural and political context (Newfield, 2009). 'Remediation' (Bolter and Grusin, 2000) denotes remaking in a different medium. Of course, these processes are not necessarily mutually exclusive. Medium and mode shift in acting out a play script (from writing to embodied modes), whilst modes shift but the medium remains constant when drawing with pencil on a page is reconfigured as writing with the same pencil on the same page. With its etymology from the Greek *sēmeîon* ('sign') from which 'semiotics' derives, 'resemioticization' suggests the process of remak-ing signs, i.e. a focus on form and meaning. This term has been coined to refer to the 'chained interplay' of 'resemiotizing moves' between contexts, practices, procedures, rules and resources, for example when an incident in a classroom was increasingly distanced in the 'recontextualization' of form-fill-ing, interactions between professionals, meetings, minutes, an official record, correspondence, and so on (Iedema, 2003).

Remaking the meanings made with the resources of one or more modes with the resources of another or others with the aim of retaining some con-stancy of meaning entails processes of interpretation, redesign and repro-duction. In 'copying', a significant proportion of signifying forms is constant between the 'original' and the 'copy' (see Chapter 2). Remaking texts across modes and media is not simply a case of straightforward swapping of one feature for another, a kind of coded slotting in. Rather, it entails complex semiotic work. Contextualized by the purpose for which the remaking is being undertaken, the material signifiers of the 'source' text are figured out. What is criterial is picked out, and decisions are reached about how best to remake meanings with the signifying resources available in the 'destination' mode. Choices and combinations of choices in the 'original' are recognized and analysed, or disregarded, and remade in re-choosing and re-combining semiotic resources with the purpose of retaining some relationality, if not constancy, of meaning. What can and cannot be done is framed by the potentialities and constraints of (socially produced) modes and the semiotic history of the remaker, as well as purpose.

MAKING WRITING INTO DRAWING

Everyday lexical resources are the common property of cultures and social groups, and meanings are made with them repeatedly. Well-acknowledged words and wording are suggestive, even directive, of certain meanings, whilst exclusive of others. For example, each of the words in the phrase 'Computers in my world' (see Chapter 5) is commonly recognized in contemporary English society. This locates their potential meanings in a largely bounded—but never fixed or finite—semiotic ball court. Even so, there is not an incontrovertible singularity of meaning in the relationship between signifier and signified. 'Computer' is a signifier resource that broadly locates meaning within certain semiotic parameters. Some aspect of 'computerness' is meant, but precisely what varies. It might be interpreted as 'kit' (e.g. monitor, processing unit, keyboard, mouse) or a 'type' of computer (e.g. a desktop as against a laptop), might be extended to include other digital technologies (e.g. mobile phones, video games, televisions, etc.) and might be generalized or specified (i.e. any computer, a particular make, my computer). Meanings made of and with words are not fixed but boundedly fluid.

Rather than writing the map title 'Computers in my world' as requested, some children chose to draw. Nouns (here 'computers', 'world'), prepositions (here 'in') and possessive adjectives (here 'my') do not exist in drawing—nor does word order. The semiotic work of transducting writing into drawing entails redesigning signs made with the combined resources of lexis, grammar, orthography or typography, punctuation, presentation and layout as signs made with the resources of line, shape, sometimes colour, orientation and arrangement. How did children handle this? Jade drew an image of the final noun ('world') first (Figure 7.1a). An outline circle superimposed with shapes of varying size and shape, some 'wrapped' over the perimeter, represents the celestial body. As precision in this context was not to do with geographical accuracy this is not inadequate, but sufficient for indicating the global. On each of the 23 land mass areas of sufficient size, Jade drew a representation that consists of a square inside a square superimposed over the uppermost point of a triangle. In the context of the map as a whole— where, albeit smaller, these images are identical to four others whose relative enlargement allowed her to represent examples of digital activities on the monitor screens—this representational economy is sufficient to denote 'computerness'. A plural noun indicates more than one, but does not enumerate how many, unless an amount is specified. How many 'computers' should be drawn? There is never more than one computer per landmass in Jade's node. This should not be interpreted literally, but as a metaphor. The one stands for the many. A single computer indicates regularity of equipment across geographical locations. It is not the exact number that is significant, but numerosity: the many places where computers can be found all around the world, or computers as a worldwide phenomenon. By combining dual-image configurations of computers and the world, Jade designed a visual metaphor.

Both writing and drawing have ways of suggesting locational relationships, but with a shift respectively between prepositions in the linearity of language and position in the spatiality of image. Jade remade the preposition 'in' of 'Computers in my world' by positioning computers inside the circular enclosure that represents the world. Sophie ingeniously combined the idea of containing and containment (Figure 7.1b). Positioned at the very centre of her map is a globe drawn on a computer screen. The computer is superimposed on a second larger globe. Sophie's drawing shows the world in the computer in the world. The outer, framing world represents the celestial body

7.1a   Jade.

7.1b   Sophie.

Figure 7.1   'Computers in my world'.

where computers are located and represents computers as a global phenomenon. The inner, screen-located world shows digital access—perhaps contact
with people and information available globally. In this double redesign of the
preposition 'in', the title is represented in its given and reversed arrangement:
'Computers in my world' and 'My world in computers'.

What is actually going on when children 'draw a picture' after they have
finished the 'work' of composing an account? This is so utterly commonplace that it is seemingly barely worthy of remark. Metaphor is one way
of signifying abstract ideas. Obtaining from similarity between two entities, there is correspondence of meaning (Van Leeuwen, 2005a: 30). With
intangible concepts and beliefs, representation cannot be based on physical

7.2a Megan.

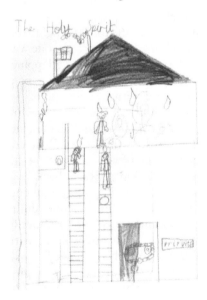

7.2b Gareth.

Figure 7.2 Pentecost.

resemblance, but derives from humanly constructed similes. The Christian festival of Pentecost celebrates the gift of the Holy Spirit, which is believed to have descended on the followers of Jesus in the form of a strong wind and tongues of fire. In a religious education lesson, Megan (age 7 years) wrote within her recount of the story 'The holy spirit looked like wind and a little fire'. How is it possible to remake in drawing the two elements of this metaphor signifying a non-physical entity?

Wind is movement of air. It cannot of itself be seen. How can things that are invisible be drawn? Children sometimes show the effects of wind as dishevelled hair, bent trees or the directionality of smoke—Peirce's 'indexicality' (Buchler, 1955: 108–109). Megan's concern was not with the causality of the meteorological phenomenon, but the wind-like quality of the Holy Spirit. Her multiply overlaid loops and swirls represent the movement of wind (Figure 7.2a). Omission of a pencil outline contrasts with that of the two co-present people, suggesting a distinction between them, perhaps the ethereality of the spirit as against the physicality of human beings.

The second part of the metaphor is fire. Fire can be seen. Gareth, who undertook the same task as Megan, wrote 'Sudnly (suddenly) the holy spirit came down in flames and a big bust (burst) of wind'. He separated the two features of the metaphor. Distributed throughout the upper room, Gareth drew flames as teardrop shapes, some touching the tops of people's heads (the gift, he wrote, that Jesus 'would send') with swirls underneath representing the eddying movement of the wind (Figure 7.2b). Megan chose to represent the Holy Spirit as one graphic entity; indeed she inscribed the union of wind and fire in a single graphic act. In the topic on light studied by Rachel, Katie and Daniel in a different school (see Chapter 3), one way in which these children drew fire was to make a series of either overlapping or separate triangles coloured orange, red and yellow. Megan's choice of peach, superimposed with orange and then overlaid with heavily applied yellow swirls signifies fire. She selected a similar colour scheme in her drawing of God and a fiery sun approximately 15 weeks earlier. Arguably, matching these colours with those of the red and yellow attire worn by Jesus—in contrast with the green shading and multicoloured dots of the robes of the 'Dispicpal (disciple)'— may imply some sort of relationship between them.

The materiality of substance provides signifying possibilities beyond line and shape to include, for example, finish (shine, dullness), depth (opacity, transparency), texture (roughness, smoothness), tactility (tackiness, indentation) and colour (shade, hue). This opens up potentialities for representing certain defining attributes of phenomena. For example, choice of the glossy finish of black felt pen was a means of representing the polished sheen of a bat's wings (Ormerod and Ivanic, 2002: 72–73). What is chosen from what is available is of note. Megan used pencil crayons to colour her pencil outlined drawings of Jesus and a disciple, but she made her representation of the Holy Spirit with wax crayon. Why did she do this? Her shift of substance had significant somatic effects not evident in the scanned reproduction. Firstly, it had a visual impact. Shining as the light caught it, the waxy veneer gave off a glossy iridescence. Movement of the head and page had the effect of changing hues and at certain angles the substance assumed an almost luminous appearance. Secondly, the image provided a different sensory experience from the drawing and writing around it. Passing the fingers over the page, Megan's representation of the Holy Spirit image had a distinctive tactility in comparison with the other textual constituents. It was smooth, unlike the indentations made by the pencil strokes, and sticky. She used substance to indicate difference, and perhaps salience. Megan seems to have been suggesting some sort of 'shining' quality, either the heat or shimmer of the Holy Spirit's fire-like quality or maybe its ethereality. At any rate, the properties of wax crayon were deemed more suited to the task of representing this complicated abstract idea than coloured pencil.

Megan's drawing of the Holy Spirit is by no means meaningless scribble. It is a sign complex. By combining the resources of line, colour and substance, she was able to represent concisely different facets of a complex theological idea originally expressed in words. Megan settled on which resources were most apt to signify her meanings and co-deployed them in an integrated act of co-generation. She made three signs simultaneously: the resource of line as overlaid loops to signify a wind-like characteristic, the resource of colour as peach superimposed with orange and yellow to signify a fire-like attribute and the resource of substance with a glossy finish to signify brilliance. The 'and' of the simile became a union of co-present features. Her drawing consists of 'wind-as-line + fire-as-colour + ethereality-as-substance = drawing of the Holy Spirit' or 'sign + sign + sign = sign complex'. Megan's representation is multiply semiotic. The integration and interdependence of form and meaning in her drawing co-construct this synthesized sign complex. Her semiotic work was deceptive in its apparent effortlessness. Indeed, this drawing is so unexceptional in its ordinariness that its significance can easily be passed by without remark. In fact, the design of this multiply semiotic economy of expression entailed complex processes of remaking as interpretation, redesign and reproduction.

These are not 'just' quick drawings, but transmodal redesigns from writing to drawing. Written designs consisting of definite and indefinite article, noun, adjective, verb, preposition and conjunction were redesigned with the lines, shapes, size, arrangement, colour and substance of drawing. Even as the children endeavoured to sustain constancy of meaning between wording and drawing in terms of subject matter, shifting between modes resulted in shifts in meaning. Features absent from the writing are specified in drawing (e.g. the components and arrangement of computer systems and the attributes of the world), lost (e.g. the possessive 'my' and the name of the Holy Spirit) and augmented (e.g. ethereality). There are constancies of meaning, but not equivalence, and there are changes, losses and additions. Different resolutions to the same task are possible. There is no one unique solution, because meanings are made, not transported wholesale—even though some redesigns might be deemed more successful than others. Each version is similar in some respects and quite different in others.

MAKING A TRANSCRIPT

The transcription of an interview planned, conducted and audio recorded for the ImpaCT2 evaluation by an 11-year-old might seem a straightforward if demanding process of 'copying down' the words that were said over the 7 minutes 22 seconds of the exchange. Actually, it entailed complex processes of interpretation, redesign and reproduction. The challenges encountered by Ella as she transcribed are a compelling reminder of the difficulties of making speech into the lettered form. Her dilemma was that the resources available in bodily produced speech and writing inscribed on a page do not entirely match. Transcription demands recognition of the continuities and disparities between source and destination modes: what is shared and what is unavailable. Decisions are reached about how meanings can be remade: what is do-able and what is not. Ella had not been inducted into the detailed and intricate methods of transcription, indeed the brief asked for a report. So how did she go about remaking an audio-recorded interview on the page?

The modes of speech and writing share the resources of language; words can be articulated or inscribed graphically. This aspect of the transcription was straightforward, if demanding. Cross-referencing with her audio recording shows Ella's 13-page transcript to be an extraordinarily accurate verbatim record. In her commitment to capturing the 'fullness' of the exchange, she painstakingly transcribed what was said word-for-word, never substituting articulated vocabulary with alternatives. Making written words look different from what might be anticipated in formal writing signals the orality of conversation. Ella re-presented speech-like lexis through spelling. All 22 instances of agreement are consistently written as 'yeah' and she repeatedly chose 'coz' rather than 'because' (which never occurs), with a single occurrence of 'coarse' (Figure 7.3a), in addition to 48 elisions including 'can't', 'it's', 'don't', 'they're' and 'wasn't' (e.g. Figure 7.3). On one occasion, 'thas' as a shortened version of the more usual written 'that's', captures the clipped pronunciation of speech. Ella interspersed these across her transcript with sufficient frequency to alert the reader that this is a graphic remaking of spoken exchange between friends.

Formal writing and everyday conversation have distinct syntactical organizations. A characteristic feature of speech is its proliferation of intricately and elaborately interwoven grammatical items (function words) in contrast with the more closely packed lexical density (content words) of writing (Chafe, 1982; Halliday, 1989: 61–75). With meticulous attention to detail, Ella did not abridge the syntax of the interview interchange; she did not omit, alter or simplify complex syntactical structures and clausal strings. Considering the challenges and complexities of word for word transcription her attention to detail is quite astounding, for example, 'thought it was a great that that didn't really, that wasn't interacting um said' (Figure 7.3b). On the first page of her transcript Ella wrote 'has bell gone'. The definite article is omitted (i.e. she did not write 'Has the bell gone?'). This

interviewee:
OK then I'll begin when, when I find my questions.

– door closes –

O.k

interviewer:
O.k din denle in den dahh!

interviewee
Do you think children should be aloud into chatrooms in case of danger, under the age of 15?

interviewer:
Well well um I watch this program named um um called a Sister sister, yeah yeah coarse it it's very very good

interviewee:
-sings- sister sister!

interviewer:
Hey you can't sing the theme song!

7.3a   Interactional exchange.

& talk with this person um they um asked if they could go over to the house but they wern't aloud so the person that wasn't having a talk thought it was a great that that didn't really, that wasn't interacting um said hey you should do this it's a one in a life time chance so she went over there instead of her and he actually asked her to go over - it would be good if I could remember which one is which and and um - I do remember which one is which but nevermind and and and up um he wasn't actually that person they found but in the end and then the other sister twin sister like me, he! he! went over there and and and - yeah but

interviewee:
haha! so -

7.3b   Ongoing contribution.

Figure 7.3   Transcription (Ella).

captures the virtual disappearance of 'the' as it precedes the crucial noun ('bell') which receives intonational and intensitive emphasis at the peak of the phrase. This is not a mistake but a remaking. Across the transcript, the hesitation 'um' occurs 55 times, that is about once very 22 words. In approximately half of these instances Ella located it with absolute accuracy, even making painstaking adjustments, as in her opening words 'is um just to find out um whether um'. Along with consecutive occurrences of 'and' (e.g. 'and and and um—I do remember which one is which but never mind—and and and up um' in Figure 7.3b), she captured the falterings, self-corrections, repetitions, restarts and restatements typical of speech. Each has its own situated meaning, for example uncertainty, thinking time, teasing, frustration and building suspense. Full stops and capital letters are notable by their scarcity. This was no accident. Disruption of what the reader would normally expect in formal writing is powerful sign making that signals the chaining of speech as successions of connected clauses. It implies that the conversation was not 'sentenced' but characterized by the continuousness of the unbroken talk of one individual (e.g. Figure 7.3b) and, elsewhere, the interweaving of the dyad.

Ella's transcript is characterized by inventiveness and initiative. In total, she included six different punctuation marks. Selecting familiar signifiers for unexpected signifieds purveyed the 'un-writing-like-ness' of speech. That she was confident with punctuating formal writing conventionally is evident in the questions of her preparatory notes, where she consistently used beginning capital letters and question marks at the end, as in 'Do you think children should be aloud (allowed) into chatrooms in case of danger, under the age of 15?' (Figure 7.3a). Quite different from everyday experience of writing in the classroom, this meant suspending some aspects of school literacy learning and re-conceiving punctuation for a new purpose. By multiplying the meanings of punctuation marks, a signifier might imply something in one position and something else somewhere else, and sometimes a different punctuation mark might be chosen for a similar function. Ambiguities and inconsistencies in her choices are not deficiencies. Rather, they signal the complexities of somehow remaking the nuances of speech on the page.

In many, even most, ways the mode of writing is inadequate to the needs of the transcriber. Some features of speech are not readily realizable on the page. The materiality of speech is sound. It is articulated in the tonicity of voice (sound quality and tone), the modulations of pitch (intonation), the crescendos and diminuendos of intensity (loudness and quietness) and variations of rhythm (tempo and pausing). Combined in complex configurations to create the phrasing of speech, these have been culturally developed over thousands of years to communicate meanings powerfully and in ways that are clearly understood. Melodic patterns and variations in phrasing, pace and volume are semiotic resources with which speakers create cadences that work in harmony with wording and that allow certain things to go unsaid. These features are entirely absent from orthography. This forces the transcriber to find means of redesign that are best suited to what the resources of writing will allow. As written text precludes the sounds, volumes and rhythms of speech, Ella was faced with the challenge of representing them in a different way. Her exclamation marks are visual indictors of cadences of auditory significance in the interview exchange: intensification of intonation, tunefulness, and shifts in rhythm and volume. Their function is to convey lively altercation (e.g. 'yeah they do!'), surprise (e.g. 'but he wasn't!'), jovial disagreement (e.g. the conjoined 'shutup!'), frustration (e.g. 'get on with it!'), resigned agreement (e.g. 'no!'), reprimand ('Hey you can't sing the theme song!'), friendly banter (e.g. 'And and so!'), a fanfare ('din denle in den dehn!' in Figure 7.3a), chanting (e.g. 'sings—Inch high priveat (private) eye yeah!') and singing (sister sister!' in Figure 7.3a). This provides information crucial to the reader's understanding of the register of the interaction.

Ella remade turn taking through layout. The proportion of marked and unmarked space to the right of the page represents speech boundaries. Continuous areas of writing represent extended individual contributions (e.g. Figure 7.3b). Rapid swapping between speakers in the fast moving pace of shorter bursts of rapid, alternating exchange can be seen at a glance in graphic density to the left of the page and large areas of white space to the right. Transcription of the linearity of one person's speech is challenging enough. Simultaneous speech is another problem entirely. Perhaps the most convoluted instance of rapid swapping between speakers and concurrent talk is about half way through the interview when the girls were discussing a slightly risqué ethical issue, where the discussion includes clarification and explanation, hesitation and agreement, assertion and counter-suggestion. Deciphering who said what and in what order presumably required backtracking and re-listening. Persisting with her chosen layout, Ella made frequent swaps between speakers, each making short, sometimes unfinished interjections. This conveys the complexity of the girls' exchange as they supported one another in their exploration of this delicate subject. More or less intense graphic coverage is an indicator of the temporal, and it is also a metaphor for the social because it shows the patterning of the girls' co-construction of meaning in this interview situation. How Ella dealt with the challenges of remaking the complexities of rapid exchange, interwoven contributions and simultaneity of a temporal mode into the spatiality of writing was principled.

In her role as transcriber, Ella went beyond recording what was said. There was no need to announce who each speaker was prior to each utterance in the face-to-face exchange of the interview event. Identity has to be dealt with differently in a transcript. Throughout, 'interviewer' and 'interviewee' (inversely of conventional usage, and consistently followed by a colon) identify the speakers not as named individuals but according to the roles they assumed in the interview situation. The reader should expect difference: that questions will be asked by the interviewer and that replies will be given by the respondent. Words have different functions: identification (from here, this is uttered by ...) and succeeding dialogic content (this is what was said ...). Hyphenation performs a semiotic function akin to stage directions in a play script: articulations such as throat clearing (e.g. '—coughs—umm yeah

I do'), bodily actions (e.g. '—nods head—'), singing ('sings—sister sister!' in Figure 7.3a) and sounds other than the girls' voices (e.g. a 9-second swishing sound following by high-pitched creaking, a pause, further creaking with an upwardly sliding pitch, a gap of around 5 seconds and then a loud bang recorded as '—door closes—' in Figure 7.3a). These marks inform the reader that the words sandwiched between dashes should be interpreted differently from the words that precede and follow: not as recorded speech but as contextual information. A parenthesized clarification that was not actually spoken provides explanatory information for the benefit of the reader (e.g. 'and—yes egg—nick name'). Implicit in Ella's transcript is her awareness of readership.

As aural matter in one place becomes graphic matter elsewhere, the discrete material entities of the original and remade texts have a separate physical existence. The audio recording is a series of signifiers that are subject to the interpretation of the listener, whilst the transcript is another series of signifiers that are subject to the interpretation of the reader. Where the redesigned text stands alone, inferences must be made about the signifiers of the source. Ella made every effort to remake the continuousness of clausal speech and the melodiousness of intonation. Similarly, the aurality of laughter proved problematic to transcribe because the resources to remake its range and diversity in writing simply do not exist ('ha ha'). These sounds took many different forms on the audio recording such as giggling, an outburst and intake of breath, nasal emission of air, suppressed chortling, whooping and vocalized guffawing. Each had its own sounds and situated meaning in the context of the exchange, for example to convey amusement, hilarity, embarrassment and uncertainty (e.g. Figure 7.3b)—with just one variation in 'he! he!' (hēhē) expressing pride in being a twin (Figure 7.3b). The reader is obliged to construe meanings through the contextualization of what comes before. Always an approximation rather than a replication of the original realization, the transcript is subject to, if not misinterpretation, alternative interpretation. As greater specificity of meaning is not possible in the written mode, the reader cannot be absolutely certain about the precise sound signified. Indeed, the boisterousness that might be inferred from the transcript alone is actually in sharp contrast with the subtlety of the interchange on the audio recording. This disjunction epitomizes the challenges of remaking the orality / aurality of sounds as speech into the visuality of marks on a page. In this respect, there is 'incommensurability' (Lemke, 1998: 110) between the modes of speech and writing.

The semiotic plenitude of the face-to-face interview became an aural selection in the audio recording that excluded modes such as gesture, posture and facial expression, as well as the setting in which it took place. Ella's record was a further selection. She made choices about what to include and what to exclude. It would have been unreasonable to include every nuance of meaning. Remaking every spoken inflection would have made her work unmanageable, and marking of the less remarkable would have cluttered the transcript. Hints here and there were sufficient. She selected what she considered worthy of marking and in sufficient quantity to indicate the sounds and rhythms of speech. Ella simultaneously analysed as she transcribed. Her semiotic criteria changed from moment to moment according to what she considered worthy of attention. The document is a record of semiotic choices made at key points in her transcription. Her spellings, repetitions and use of punctuation are not mistakes. Ella's account provides traces of her theorization.

MAKING A STOP-FRAME ANIMATION FROM A STORYBOARD

Stop-frame animation is suggested in the Primary Framework for 5- to 7-year-olds in English schools as a means of 'add(ing) value to aspects of literacy learning' (DCFS, 1997). Located under the strand of 'engaging with and responding to texts', it is described as a way of supporting literacy learning as students 'create a visual adaptation of a simple text' (ibid.). In the Test Bed programme that promoted computers in education, 6-year-olds visited a neighbouring school in order to learn how to make a stop-frame animation, with the aim of returning and teaching their classmates in a peer tutoring initiative. Given plastic small world play figures, groups negotiated a story orally and then collaboratively produced a storyboard as the plan for subsequent movie making. The children had no previous knowledge or experience of animation. In prior discussion, the class was in unanimous agreement that Wallace and Gromit—characters made from modelling clay featuring in a popular series of British animated films—are not real, but thought either that they are puppets or robots, or that there is 'a person inside'. Framed by the achievements deemed possible within limited time constraints, the children were set the task of making short action-only sequences, a precursor to animated movies that include soundtrack, background music, synchronized speech, title, subtitles and credits (Burn and Durran, 2007: 43–63; Marsh, 2004). What processes of redesign are entailed in remaking as stop-frame animation the signs made in the writing and drawing of a storyboard?

Character is a key feature of stories. Allocated three small world plastic figures, attribution of identity was compelled by their appearance. The monkey was taken as it was without debate, although its role in the storyline had not yet been considered. Variations in the clothing of human figures (e.g. the type and colour of garments; presence or absence of a hat and its shape), bodily attributes (e.g. hair length, style and colour; the presence or absence of a moustache) and relative size (approximately 5cm or 8cm) evoked the imagination of possibilities for the ascription of character. Decisions were made about who each figure should be based on the appropriateness or distinctiveness of their 'look'. A broad-rimmed hat and trousers tucked into knee-length boots were together sufficient to be suggestive of 'pirateness'. On the basis of this resolution, the smaller, less distinctive figure, without a hat and clothed in a red tunic, was also imagined to be a pirate (perhaps the ship's boy?). Identity in the wordlessness of action-only stop-frame animation required that the distinguishing features of small world figures were adequate of themselves to be sufficiently well understood by the viewer. This was helped along by an orally supplied title; Ebony announced that the movie was going to be called 'The pirates and the monkey'. A serendipitously discovered painting used as a backdrop for the animation—sea with waves; sky with sun, clouds and birds; and an island with a beach and a palm tree—provided a location that gave an additional clue to the identity of the human characters.

In developing the storyboard collaboratively, these identities were realized in a multimodal ensemble of writing and drawing. Given limited time for their planning, Kelsey instructed, 'Draw them as fast as you can (.) you don't have to draw them properly.' The speed of production inhibited the kind of specifying attributes that would be needed in a more enduring and self-sufficient text such as a piece of curricular work as against a temporary reference sheet. Even so, the characters had to be readily identifiable. The monkey is differentiated by its elliptical ears in every occurrence, and one member of the group distinguished between the two pirates by including or omitting a hat (frames 3, 4 and 5 in Figure 7.4). Naming ('the pirates' twice and 'the monkey' three time) 'anchors' (Barthes, 1977: 39) identity that might not be immediately obvious from image alone.

In the representational mode switching of redesigning the storyboard as an animation, the aim was to sustain constancy between what had been drawn and written and the action of the movie. The children took the prior framing of the storyboard seriously, constantly referring back to it to check what had been done and what was needed next. This extract

Figure 7.4   The storyboard (Ebony, Ambareen and Jeselle).

from the video summary is taken from about half way through movie making:

> 'Now,' says Ebony. 'What was next? We need the paper.' She disappears to find the storyboard. On her return, Ebony rights and repositions the monkey that Ambareen and Jeselle have knocked over. She then prises the two pirate figures from Jeselle, protesting, 'Oh don't put it there, no, no, no, no, no, no, no.' Ebony looks intently at the storyboard, then, grasping the two pirates in her right hand, rehearses their movement towards the monkey as she reads aloud, 'They find the monkey.' Dangling the figures between her fingers, she continues to read the next caption: 'The pirates are cross.' Jeselle points to this frame on the storyboard and then to the succeeding one, which Ebony attends to with concentration, and they engage in some discussion. Turning back to the 'stage' as she examines the storyboard, Ebony concludes 'Okay we've done that bit', and continues to study the page intently, presumably with a view to what comes next.

Written narratives are highly valued in education. In literacy lessons, Key Stage One children in English schools (5 to 7-year-olds) are taught how to write stories with clear sequencing—often structured as a beginning, middle and end—and to use 'adventurous and wide-ranging vocabulary' (DfEE and QCA, 1999: 48). In the shift from their habituated experience of story writing to the entirely unfamiliar mode of action-only animation, the children were restricted by the potentialities of a representational mode with different and comparatively reduced affordances:

Di: What do you normally do when you make up a story?
Kelsey: Write.
Di: So how was today different?
Kelsey: It was because you move it and we don't usually do that (*appealing to the rest of the group*) we write don't we?

Redesigning a narrative as action-only animation limited these 6-year-olds to the semiotic possibilities of the small world figures and the technology (a webcam and computer software). Certain options were open to them whilst others were not. The semiotic work in which the children engaged was to discover the signifying properties of the spatio-temporal resources of action-only stop-frame animation, and to investigate the meanings they could make with them.

The children were compelled by which bits of the small world play figures could move and how. Jointing at the waist enabled movement between a standing and sitting position, and the heads could rotate full-circle. Each arm moved on an (almost) 180-degree vertical plane from against the body to above the head. The legs were not separately hinged. Based on what the children had experienced through handling and manipulation earlier on in the lesson and previously beyond school, this framed the meanings that could be made. The challenge for the animators was how their narrative could be redesigned with these movements alone. Decisions had to be made about what could be done and what could not. They came to realize that walking could not be simulated by putting one leg in front of the other, but had to be construed from the forward motion of the whole figure. This could not be achieved in real time, but had to be broken down into multiple, measured moves of small distances with each successive repositioning recorded to produce a single frame in the movie. As they practised shooting a scene, Ebony and Ambareen created rhythmic walking with corresponding raising and lowering of arms, carefully synchronized with regard to pace so that one pirate following the other was kept an even distance. Laughing, Ebony advised her tutees the following day, 'Move it a little step (.) otherwise it will just go bouncing.' Systematic moves required care, concentration and patience, and occupied much of the movie-making time. Through their experience, the children came to understand that the extended timeframes of the process of production, which they measured in relation to morning break and lunch time, became temporally condensed in movie playback time. The 37 frames of one sequence took around 5 minutes to compose and produced just 5 seconds of movie.

Sequentiality of narrative was not new for these children who read and wrote stories, watched films and cartoons, and played digital games. The storyboard obliged them to break down their narratives into a succession of scenes. A large (A3) sheet of plain white paper folded three times to create equally proportioned graphic divisions was a device for breaking down the plot. However, the movie was an ongoing, connected sequence as moves, actions and episodes merged in a rolling continuousness. What could be postponed, even bypassed, in the linearity of the separate frames of the storyboard must be filled in as uninterrupted movement in the movie, such as walking back to the boat, boarding and exiting in the final two frames of the storyboard (Figure 7.4). Achieving flow is a feature of successful animation absent from the drawing and writing of a storyboard. Ongoing action had to be envisioned in the process of production as the children imagined the final outcome. They came to appreciate that lifting figures and putting them down in a different place disrupted smoothness, and that moving the camera midstream could dislocate continuity in the length and angle of shot. It was well understood that the task was to make it appear that the figures were moving by themselves. In reviewing their movies, the children realized that any appearance of the animators would detract from the effect for which they were aiming. Dean commented, 'When it moves and your hands weren't in there it looks like it was doing it by itself' and Ebony later made this explicit in peer teaching, instructing her tutees, 'Remember if she says shoot and her hands are in the way you can't press it until her hands have gone.' Putting their hands on the table, behind their backs or to their cheeks whilst calling out 'shoot' became a way of displaying readiness for a shot to be taken, and this stringent rule was frequently enforced by the children (Table 7.1).

Three main features of the plot are identified in the writing and drawing of the storyboard: searching (the mystery), finding (the dilemma) and sailing away (the resolution). How could this be remade in action-only animation? Searching was pivotal to the opening of the story. The temporality of the verb with its subject and anticipated object in the written sentence 'two pirates look for treasher (treasure)' was written rapidly. In small world enactment, this was choreographed as figures moving through space and time. Combining movement, direction, pace and pausing required attendance to features in the movie that were not necessary in writing. As in the drawing of the first frame, side-by-side positioning of the two human plastic figures established an existing friendship or collegiality between the two pirates as they embarked on a shared enterprise. (Face-to-face orientation would have suggested an exchange between the two characters). In order to distinguish between 'going towards' and 'searching', the girls took up the teacher's suggestion of a snaking route in order to indicate indeterminacy. This implied uncertainty created tension in the unfolding of the act of searching. Choreography demanded attendance to different units of text: interrelationships between the smallest adjustments and combinations of adjustments as the children created momentary detail within the framing of a more extended action, located in the unfolding of an episode.

The negation of the written statement 'they don't find the treasher (treasure)' in the storyboard was created in the movie by the addition of a prop. This supplied an essential meaning that could not otherwise be created in action-only animation. A cross cut out from paper and placed underneath the monkey was sufficient of itself without any further need

Table 7.1 Checking the Screen (plain = Ebony; italics = Ambareen)

Action (left hand)	Gaze	Speech	Time
elbow resting on the table, lowers her hand towards her figure	own figure		1 second
hesitates and withdraws her hand	screen		
	own figure		
forearm flat on the table, grasps her figure with her index finger and thumb	screen		1 second
moves her figure towards Ambareen's *moves figure towards Ebony's*			2 seconds
releases her figure	figures		1 second
raises her hand to her face	screen	*shoot!*	

for explanation: 'X marks the spot' is a culturally well-known metaphor for the site of buried treasure. Placing the monkey at a distance and at the opposite side from the pirates' oblique point of entry and facing the camera was a means of disconnection indicating the, as yet, unfamiliar and unknown. Seated motionless on the cross, the monkey was introduced by its presence and backgrounded by its stillness. As yet unnoticed by the pirates, its significance for the development of the storyline remained yet to be revealed. A key feature in the humour of the story was the unexpected: the pirates found a monkey instead of treasure. As such, searching with a hint of what was being searched for was suggestive of what was yet to come and a way of building suspense.

Remaking the meanings of the storyboard as action-only animation entailed attendance to what was going on in the development of the plot, and also how comprehensible this would be for the viewer. This demanded simultaneous 'mapping' of the 'ideational' and the 'interpersonal' (Halliday, 1978: 50) as the girls constructed relationships between the characters and with their audience. In visualising what the viewer would see in the finished movie, Ebony frequently monitored the real-time shot displayed on the screen (e.g. Table 7.1). With a view to flow, the tools of the digital medium provided further opportunities to refine the movies. For example, in dragging and dropping each frame one by one the following day, Ebony instructed her tutees to remove an instance of a hand appearing in shot ('Delete the hand (.) delete the hand'). Playback was approached with great excitement as the animators evaluated the effectiveness of their designs (e.g. Ebony enthused, 'Let's see if they shake hands!').

Some kinds of explicitness possible in the storyboard could not be easily realized—or realized at all—given the material attributes of the small world figures. The affective and attitudinal (being cross, making friends and living happily ever after) are key features of the storyboard plot. As the girls rehearsed the opening of their movie, they had not yet realized that the resource of speech would not be available. Ebony, who took on the role of director as well as narrator, insisted on angry intonation for the chief pirate's speech in response to finding a monkey instead of treasure. This demanded subsequent transmodal and transmedial redesign. Representing anger in the written narrative 'The pirates are cross' shown in drawing as down-turned mouths and angled eyebrows (the fourth frame of the storyboard) was problematic with the fixed facial expressions of the figures (as against the potentialities of malleable materials such as modelling clay or dough) and in the absence of greater articulation (jointing at the knee would have enabled foot-stamping). On the other hand, 'they Mack frands (make friends) with the monkey' (the fifth frame of the storyboard) could be enacted, and the children did this through proximity and hand shaking. Albeit sustaining broad constancy of character and plot, the movie sequences were redesigns of the storyboard where some meanings were sustained, some were reconfigured, some were lost and some were added.

DISCUSSION

Remaking texts across modes and media is not replication. It is a process of resemioticization that entails the interpretation, redesign and reproduction of form and meaning. Like all text making, transmodal / transmedial remaking is principled, and is framed by what is being done and why, who it is for and how it will be used. Ella took the job of reporting to be transcription, which she undertook with meticulous attention to detail in ways that she considered fitting to the task brief. The movie makers took seriously their storyboard in the making of their animation, with a concern for what the viewer would see and so how the storyline would be understood. These decisions make interwoven epistemological, social and representational demands: which features of the 'source' texts are selected, and how they are changed or supplemented; communication with an 'audience' and how social relations are sustained or reshaped; and how shifts across modes, multimodal ensembles and media are handled.

Remaking one text as another across modes and media is concerned with the *textus*—the interweaving—of semiotic resources in the interpretation and reshaping of meaning. From the range of semiotic features that co-exist and co-function in the 'source' text the remaker figures out complexes of form and meaning, and remakes these as other complexes of form and meaning in semiotic features that co-exist and co-function in the 'destination' text. Decisions are made about what can be achieved, and what cannot. Some features are selected, others omitted and others added. Some meanings may be abandoned because they are not essential, because they are not easily do-able, or because they are not possible. What could be left vague or ambiguous may be specified. Shaped by the task to be done, the interest of the remaker and the resources available, resolutions are reached about what will feature, what will be approximated and what will be put aside. The outcome is a text where certain constancies of meaning are sustained, but whose signifying forms differ from their source in readily recognizable ways, with implications for meaning.

Much is known about some kinds of text making, whilst others have attracted relatively minor attention. Remaking texts, something done by children as a matter of course, is fraught with complexity as they manage constancies and dissonances between modes and media, and their potentialities and constraints. On the one hand, it is surprising that children handle some of these semiotic complexities with apparent ease. On the other, it is unsurprising that they find aspects challenging. The semiotic work entailed in redesign is remarkable, and yet it passes by largely unnoticed because of its very ordinariness. What it means to remake meaning across modes is not on the current agenda of schools—indeed drawing in response to writing and making stop-frame animation are generally considered to be subsidiary to the 'real' work of the curriculum. Even if not valued, or at any rate valued less, this does not diminish the semiotic effort children invest in the resemioticization of remaking one text into another.

8   From the Unremarkable to the Remarkable

If a deficit view of texts that are 'just brief', 'just fleeting', 'just a mess', 'just repetition', 'just copying', 'just a waste of time' or 'just plain wrong' gives way to recognition of children's investment of semiotic work, the focus moves to what they can do and the principles they bring to their text making. It marks a shift from shortcoming and randomness to agency, resourcefulness and purposiveness.

RECOGNITION AND IDEOLOGY

Entirely ordinary, as children interpret and document their everyday world, they make meaning in a multiplicity of ways. Recognition emerges as an essential feature of the semiotic work of text making. Drawing and writing entail interpretation of what is needed, judgements about fitness for purpose and resolution with regard to how to proceed. This includes analysis of stable and shifting criteria: in subject matter, social relations and representational resources. Redesigning existing texts (in 'copying' or transmodally) and integrating aspects of prior representation and communication demands recognition of what is needed from what is given within the framing of specified purposes. As a matter of course, children figure out what they deem to be suitable, consider options, resolve difficulties, imagine alternatives and plan ahead. From the complex and ongoing flow of semiosis, their texts represent a semiotic settling on what is deemed apt. The apparently unremarkable becomes remarkable.

Ideologically shaped, what is and is not recognized in children's texts is framed by relations of power. Evaluation of sufficiency may be more or less explicit, but it is always there. Endeavouring to understand children's drawing and writing from their view of the world may unsettle what is taken for granted, in part because it may not conform to the expectations of others. Serious engagement with children's everyday text making shows respect for their investment of semiotic work, and this shifts the focus from defectiveness or immaturity to discernible principles. If the variety of ways in which meanings are made is not acknowledged, then evaluation—as interpretation and response—may be at best partial, even misguided, and at worst unjust. Providing appropriate and constructive feedback that is relevant and respectful has implications for time: time to observe interactions around text making, time to ponder, time to discuss, time to look beyond to other forms of text making and time to explore together.

An objection to an approach to classroom texts that endeavours to recognize a variety of ways in which children make meaning might be that it is all very well but, if it falls outside what is recognized in the dominant discourses and practices of schooling, it is irrelevant. In other words, what is the point of bringing attention to the semiotic range of children's drawing and writing if this is not specified in curricula or subject to assessment? Firstly, taking seriously social justice in an increasingly pluricultural world, there are implications for accommodating the diversity of resources children have at their disposal. Secondly, accepting that school discourses and practices are not the only discourses and practices acknowledges representational shifts across social environments, and accords them respect in their own place. Thirdly, longstanding dominant discourses exert such a powerful influence that they become unquestioned orthodoxy. Critical reflection on and debate around what is taken for granted provides a space for re-seeing what is commonly accepted, and even ground for challenging contemporary policy, pedagogical practices and forms of assessment—not as an end in itself, but as a means of engaging with issues in contemporary education, reconfirming what is valued and, with well-substantiated and wide approval, initiating change.

Recognizing the remarkable in the unremarkable—in features that pass by unnoticed and in 'mistakes'—does not mean abandoning what is valued educationally. Discourses that call for a return 'back to basics' represent a justifiable political and societal concern that people should be literate and numerate (or should have the opportunity to make an informed choice not to be). We want children to be able to read and write with assurance for a range of formal purposes: to spell and punctuate with confidence and in ways apt to different genres, to experience what it is like to create a variety of texts—to write as a scientist or an historian or a poet. Competent writing is essential to educational success. It is also important for fulfilment in children's everyday lives beyond school as they seek out, engage with, make and exchange texts. Although we cannot foresee what it will mean to be literate in the more distant future, or the role literacy will play in people's working lives, we can be fairly certain that, at least in the near future, it will retain an essential role in the everyday world and a key feature of certain employment prospects.

Drawing is learned more or less informally as children engage with the images they encounter in their everyday lives, as they experiment and as they observe what others do. Educational discourse positions drawing as a mode of representation largely inadequate to the needs of the curriculum, and offering little to the representation of learning in comparison with writing.

Teachers frequently support children in their writing, but tend to 'let them get on with it' when they draw. This places and displaces value. By no means is this to argue that image should surpass writing. Rather, drawing has a place for the representation of certain phenomena and relations between them, and hence for the construction and demonstration of certain aspects of knowledge and learning. Recognizing the range of semiotic features in what children draw can enable educationalists and researchers to make sound decisions about where it can be a powerful resource for representation. If knowledge and understanding of, and investigation into the potentialities of drawing were to feature more fully in initial and ongoing professional development, educationalists might be better equipped to design tasks, to engage with the meanings children make and to assess their learning.

HANDLING CHANGE

That the primacy of writing is challenged, even dislodged, by the arrival of digital technologies is becoming a familiar assertion (e.g. Bolter, 1998: 7–9; Snyder, 2001: 41). The dynamic narratives of electronic games are image dominated. Web pages, especially those frequented and made by children, are a mix of image and writing. Mobile devices not only enable talk, but also offer opportunities for texting, access to the web, the ability to capture, display and share still and moving images, and the storage and playback of music. Increasingly, whole-class digital technologies have been installed in primary schools in England (Gillen et al., 2007; Kennewell, et al., 2008; Lewin et al., 2009; Miller and Glover, 2002; Smith, Hardman and Higgins, 2006), and this has implications for the kinds of texts children encounter on a day-to-day basis in the classroom. Writing no longer inevitably dictates the layout of the screen, nor does it necessarily take on the greater share of the semiotic load. As written text becomes one means of representation amongst others, and not always the principal mode, there are implications for intermodal balance and interrelationships. On the other hand, writing in all its manifold diversity continues to be essential for certain expressions of meaning. It is not necessarily that writing is under threat or that the page is being displaced by the screen, but that children in the twenty first century are experiencing a growing array of semiotic variations.

Intense social, economic, political and technological change in recent times has undone prior stabilities. This is likely indicator of what is to come, at least in the near future. Children, as children and as they become adolescents and adults, will need to sustain flexibility to adapt to this changing representational and communicational world. This demands an open semiotic disposition that can adjust to change, and discrimination in being able to decide when one means of representation is appropriate as against another. Whatever the future holds, people will continue to need to know how to make sense of and create a range of texts. Whilst, to some extent, this might happen incidentally in children's everyday experience, there are educational implications. In order to prepare children for the future, curriculum planners need to take account of the changing forms and functions of representation and communication and policy makers need to allow time for exploring them. If children's text making is to be apt to the diversity of their current everyday lives and suitable preparation for the uncertainties of the future, they will need support in understanding the potentialities and aptness of the semiotic resources of different modes and media for particular purposes.

PEDAGOGIC ENABLING

Recognizing and valuing the signs children make in their design of classroom texts provides opportunities for identifying their pathways towards attainment targets as specified in curricular policy documents.

> 'The point of intersection between honouring what children know and pushing their boundaries is just what teaching is all about' (Bearne, 2003: 99).

In a packed day, there is little time to deliberate on why individuals might have made the signs they did, and to explore this with them. Classrooms are busy places, and teachers cannot possibly track every nuance of children's meaning making. Although they do circulate, they simply cannot be present to observe all processes of production, and it is inevitable that significant semiotic moments, which sometimes happen over just a few moments, are missed. Even so, opportunities to pause, analyse and reflect would provide space to allow teachers to engage with children's meaning making, and would to enable children to re-engage with their own texts and to examine those made by others. Formative assessment of learning is concerned with supporting learners in ways that are relevant and enabling. If assessment for learning is taken seriously, and if children's designs are taken to be principled, careful examination of the signs they have made and exploring their texts with them can provide the basis for recognizing what they have done and why, with opportunities for insights into their learning. Debate around what was done and the semiotic potentialities of different kinds of representational resources with exemplification of conventional ways of representing might constitute the ground for expansion of children's semiotic reservoirs—the 'where now' and 'where next' of responsive pedagogy.

In England, as in other countries across the world, prescribed curricular content and pedagogic practices, whilst closing down an educational period when schools and teachers could freely create their own curricula, has imposed rather rigid strictures on what is done and how. Different kinds of tasks provide different degrees of openness and constraint. Of course, it is critical that children are given instruction and directed tasks that enable them to learn how to create different kinds of texts for different purposes—and they are always agentive, even when they undertake highly constraining tasks such as the drill of repeatedly writing out words for the purpose of memorizing spelling patterns. Even so, such exercises must be balanced with opportunities to imagine and experiment. Unless from the youngest age children are given some degree of freedom in directed tasks, as well as the experience of framing their own self-initiated and self-directed projects, opportunities to assume responsibility are restricted. Taken seriously, this is not an optional add-on, but essential for fostering semiotic dispositions suited to the diversity of the contemporary world of representation and communication.

FOSTERING POSITIVE SEMIOTIC DISPOSITIONS

The capacity to approach representation confidently requires opportunities to explore and experiment, to succeed and to be challenged, to reflect and to engage in debate with others. Developing reflexivity, criticality and discernment is not just a case of locating and identifying features of texts, but also describing, analysing and critiquing their form and function. For example, hypertextual links are not neutral or value free; they construct connections that carry the values, interests and assumptions of the designers who created them (Burbules, 1998: 118–119). Analysis of how gender, relationships, race and so on are realized in image provides children with a means of examining their own beliefs and values, and those of others (Albers, Frederick and Cowan, 2009). In different cultures and in increasingly pluricultural societies, this demands recognition of and respect for diversity and alternative viewpoints (Kalantzis, Cope and Harvey, 2003). Giving children opportunities to describe, explain and analyse their own texts and those made by others can enable them to engage with different ideologies. It can also facilitate developing the capacity to shape their own social and representational futures (Kress, 1995). This is not a recommendation that yet further additions be made to an already overloaded curriculum, but rather a reorientation. One possibility is for teachers and children to share a 'metalanguage' that provides a means for discussing the design of texts (Unsworth, 2006; Zammit and Downes, 2002). Any 'curricularization' of criticality and reflexivity that has as its aim the mastery of rigid rules and procedures around the semiotics of text is self-defeating. Sensitivity to the diversity of social and cultural, and generic and discursive, frames means embracing, understanding and responding thoughtfully and judiciously to texts made by oneself and others in order to open up, not close down, debate. Occasions to air one's own views, to encounter alternative opinions, to agree and to dissent are vital to being an assured text maker.

Recognizing and taking seriously the semiotic work children invest in their drawing and writing frames how their efforts are received. As a society, we want children to aspire to success, to be productive and to be fulfilled. Means to engage critically and imaginatively in the production of a range of texts can provide the ground for being curious, for being open to innovation, for being brave enough to take action and for being willing to take risks. Nurturing positive text-making dispositions that are full of initiative, confidence and openness can enable children to participate in the world responsibly and with dignity.

References

Adami, E. (2009) 'We/youTube': exploring sign-making in video-interaction', *Visual Communication* 8(4): 379–399.

Albers, P., Frederick, T. and Cowan, K. (2009) 'Features of gender: an analysis of the visual texts of third grade children', *Journal of Early Childhood Literacy* 9(9): 234–260.

Alexander, R. (ed.) (2010) *Children, Their World, Their Education: Final Report and Recommendations of the Cambridge Primary Review*, London: Routledge.

Anning, A. (1999) 'Learning to draw and drawing to learn', *Journal of Art and Design Education* 18(2): 163–172.

Arizpe, E. and Styles, M. (2003) *Children Reading Pictures: Interpreting Visual Texts*, London: RoutledgeFalmer.

Arnheim, R. (1969) *Visual Thinking*, Berkeley, California: University of California Press.

Barrs, M. (1988) 'Maps of play', in M. Meek and C. Mills (eds.) *Language and Literacy in the Primary School* (pp. 101–115), London: Falmer Press.

Barthes, R. (1977) *Image, Music, Text* (trans. S. Heath), London: Fontana Press.

Barton, D., Hamilton, M. and Ivanic, R. (eds.) (2000) *Situated Literacies: Reading and Writing in Context*, London: Routledge.

Bearne, E. (2003) 'Rethinking literacy: communication, representation and text', *Reading, Literacy and Language* 37(3): 98–103.

Bearne, E., Ellis, S., Graham, L., Hulme, P. and Merchant, G. (2004) *More Than Words: Multimodal Texts in the Classroom*, London: Qualifications and Curriculum Authority.

Bezemer, J. and Kress, G. (2008) 'Writing in multimodal texts: a social semiotic account of designs for learning', *Written Communication* 25(2): 166–195.

Bissex, G. L. (1980) *GNYS AT WRK: A Child Learns to Write and Read*, Cambridge, Massachusetts: Harvard University Press.

Bolter, J. D. (1998) 'Hypertext and the question of visual literacy', in D. Reinking, M. C. McKenna, L. D. Labbo and R. D. Kieffer (eds.) *Handbook of Literacy and Technology: Transformations in a Post-Typographic World* (pp. 3–13), Mahwah, New Jersey: Lawrence Erlbaum Associates.

Bolter, J. D. and Grusin, R. (2000) *Remediation: Understanding New Media*, Cambridge, Massachusetts: The MIT Press.

Brittain, W. L. (1979) *Creativity, Art and the Young Child*, New York: Macmillan Publishing.

Buchler, J. (ed.) (1955) *Philosophical Writings of Peirce*, New York: Dover Publications.

Buckham, J. (1994) 'Teachers' understanding of children's drawing', in C. Aubrey (ed.) *The Role of Subject Knowledge in the Early Years of Schooling* (pp.133–167), London: The Falmer Press.

Burbules, N. C. (1998) 'Rhetorics of the web: hyperreading and critical literacy', in I. Snyder (ed.) *Page to Screen: Taking Literacy into the Electronic Era* (pp. 102–122), London: Routledge.

Burn, A. and Durran, J. (2007) *Media Literacy in Schools: Practice, Production and Progression*, London: Paul Chapman Publishing.

Burnett, C., Dickinson, P., Myers, J. and Merchant, G. (2006) 'Digital connections: transforming literacy in the primary school', *Cambridge Journal of Education* 36(1): 11–29.

Buzan, T. (1993) *The Mind Map Book: Radiant Thinking—The Major Evolution in Human Thought*, London: BBC Books.

Carrington, V. (2004) 'Texts and literacies of the Shi Jinrui', *British Journal of Sociology in Education* 25(2): 215–228.

———. (2005) 'New textual landscapes: information and early literacy', in J. Marsh (ed.) *Popular Culture, New Media and Digital Literacy in Early Childhood* (pp. 13–27), London: Routledge.

Chafe, W. L. (1982) 'Integration and involvement in speaking, writing, and oral literature', in D. Tannen (ed.) *Spoken and Written Language: Exploring Orality and Literacy* (pp. 35–53), Norwood, New Jersey: Ablex.

Christensen, P. and James, A. (2000) 'Childhood diversity and commonality: some methodological insights', in P. Christensen and A. James (eds.) *Research with Children: Perspectives and Practices* (pp. 160–178), London: Falmer Press.

Cifuentes, L. and Hsieh, Y. C. J. (2004) 'Visualization for middle school students' engagement in science learning', *Journal of Computers in Mathematics and Science Teaching* 23(2): 109–137.

Clanchy, M. T. (1993) *From Memory to Written Record: England 1066–1307* (2nd ed.), Oxford: Blackwell Publishing.

Coates, E. (2002) ''I forgot the sky!' Children's stories contained within their drawings', *International Journal of Early Years Education* 10(1): 21–35.

Collerson, J. (1986) 'Copying and composing: text and context in children's informational writing', *Educational Review* 38(2): 139–150.

Court, E. (1992) 'Researching social influences in the drawings of rural Kenyan children', in D. Thistlewood (ed.) *Research Design and Development* (pp. 51–67), Harlow: Longman.

Cox, M. (1992) *Children's Drawings*, London: Penguin Books.

Cox, R. (ed.) (2008) *The Culture of Copying in Japan: Critical and Historical Perspectives*, London: Routledge.

Cox, S. (2005) 'Intention and meaning in young children's drawing', *Journal of Art and Design Education* 24(2): 115–125.

Crawford, K., Neve, L., Pearson, M. and Somekh, B. (1999) *Creative Tensions and Disrupted Routines: The Impact of the Internet on Primary Children's Understanding of the World*, paper presented at the British Educational Research Association (BERA) Conference, University of Brighton, UK (September, 1999).

DCFS (1997) *The National Strategies: ICT Applications in Literacy—Key Stage 1*, Department for Children, Families and Schools. Available at: http://national-strategies.standards.dcsf.gov.uk/node/47640 (accessed 3 January 2009).

DfEE and QCA (1999) *The National Curriculum: Handbook for Primary Teachers in England Key Stages 1 and 2*, London: Department for Education and Employment and Qualifications and Curriculum Authority.

DfES (2006) *Primary National Strategy: Primary Framework for Literacy and Mathematics*, London: Department for Education and Skills.

Downes, T. (2002) 'Children's and families' use of computers in Australian homes', *Contemporary Issues in Early Childhood* 13(2): 182–196.

Duncum, P. (1989) 'To copy or not to copy: a review', *Studies in Art Education: A Journal of Issues and Research* 29(4): 203–210.

Dyson, A. H. (2008) 'Coach Bombay's kids learn to write: children's appropriation of media material for school literacy', in M. Mackey (ed.) *Media Literacies: Major Themes in Education* (pp. 235–275), London: Routledge.

Facer, K. (2003) *Screenplay: Children and Computing in the Home*, London: RoutledgeFalmer.

Ferrara, K., Brunner, H. and Whittemore, G. (1991) 'Interactive written discourse as an emergent register', *Written Communication* 8(1): 8–34.

Finnegan, R. (2002) *Communicating: The Multiple Modes of Human Interconnection*, London: Routledge.

Flewitt, R. (2005) 'Is every child's voice heard? Researching the different ways 3-year-old children communicate and make meaning at home and in a preschool playgroup', *Early Years* 25(3): 207–222.

Forman, G. (1998) 'Multiple symbolization in the long jump project', in C. Edwards, L. Gandini and G. Forman (eds.) *The Hundred Languages of Children: The Reggio Emilia Approach to Early Childhood Education* (2nd ed.) (pp. 171–188), Norwood, New Jersey: Ablex.

Foucault, M. (1981) 'The order of discourse' (trans. I. McLeod), in R. Young (ed.) *Untying the Text: A Post-Structuralist Reader* (pp. 48–78), London: Routledge and Kegan Paul.

Freeman, N. H. and Janikoun, R. (1972) 'Intellectual realism in children's drawings of a familiar object with distinctive features', *Child Development* 43: 1116–1121.

Gardner, H. (1980) *Artful Scribbles*, London: Jill Norman.

———. (1984) *Frames of Mind: The Theory of Multiple Intelligences* (2nd ed.), London: Fontana Press.

Gee, J. P. (1996) *Social Linguistics and Literacies: Ideology in Discourses* (2nd ed.), London: RoutledgeFalmer.

———. (2000) 'The new literacy studies: from 'socially situated' to the work of the social', in D. Barton, M. Hamilton and R. Ivanic (eds.) *Situated Literacies: Reading and Writing in Context* (pp. 180–196), London: Routledge.

———. (2003) 'Opportunity to learn: a language-based perspective on assessment', *Assessment in Education* 10(1): 27–46.

Gillen, J., Kleine Staarman, J., Littleton, K., Mercer, N. and Twiner, A. (2007) 'A 'learning revolution'? Investigating pedagogic practice around interactive whiteboards in British primary classrooms', *Learning, Media and Technology* 32(3): 243–256.

Golomb, C. (1974) *Young Children's Sculpture and Drawing: A Study in Representational Development*, Cambridge, Massachusetts: Harvard University Press.

———. (1999) 'Art and the young: the many faces of representation', *Visual Arts Research* 25(1): 27–50.

Goodnow, J. (1977) *Children's Drawing*, London: Fontana Press.

Goodnow, J. J. and Friedman, S. (1972) 'Orientations in children's human figure drawings: an aspect of graphic language', *Developmental Psychology* 7: 10–16.

Goodwin, C. (2000) 'Action and embodiment within situated human interaction', *Journal of Pragmatics* 32: 1489–1522.

Halliday, M. A. K. (1978) *Language as Social Semiotic: The Social Interpretation of Language and Meaning*, London: Edward Arnold.

———. (1989) *Spoken and Written Language* (2nd ed.), Oxford: Oxford University Press.

Halliday, M. A. K. and Hasan, R. (1976) *Cohesion in English*, London: Longman.

Heath, S. B. (1983) *Ways with Words: Language, Life, and Work in Communities and Classrooms*, Cambridge: Cambridge University Press.

Hodge, R. and Kress, G. (1988) *Social Semiotics*, Cambridge: Polity Press.

Holloway, S. H. and Valentine, G. (2003) *Cyberkids: Children in the Information Age*, London: RoutledgeFalmer.

Holm Hopperstadt, M. (2008a) 'How children make meaning through drawing and play', *Visual Communication* 7(1): 77–96.

———. (2008b) 'Relationships between children's drawing and accompanying peer interaction in teacher-initiated drawing sessions', *International Journal of Early Years Education* 16(2): 133–150.

Hull, G. and Schultz, K. (2001) 'Literacy and learning out of school: a review of theory and research', *Review of Educational Research* 71(4): 575–611.

Hutchby, I. and Moran-Ellis, J. (1998) 'Situating children's social competence', in I. Hutchby and J. Moran-Ellis (eds.) *Children and Social Competence: Arenas of Action* (pp. 7–26), London: Falmer Press.

Iedema, R. (2003) 'Multimodality, resemioticization: extending the analysis of discourse as multi-semiotic practice', *Visual Communication* 2(1): 29–57.

Jakobson, R. and Halle, M. (1956) *Fundamentals of Language*, The Hague: Mouton and Co.

James, A., Jenks, C. and Prout, A. (1998) *Theorizing Childhood*, Cambridge: Polity Press.

Jarvis, T., Hargreaves, L. and Comber, C. (1997) 'An evaluation of the role of email in promoting science investigative skills in primary rural schools in England', *Research in Science Education* 27(2): 223–236.

Kalantzis, M., Cope, B. and Harvey, A. (2003) 'Assessing multiliteracies and the new basics', *Assessment in Education* 10(1): 15–26.

Kenner, C. (2000a) 'Recipes, alphabets and I♥U: a four year old explores the visual potential of literacy', *Early Years* 20(2): 68–79.

———. (2000b) 'Symbols make texts: a social semiotic analysis of writing in a multilingual nursery', *Written Language and Literacy* 3(2): 235–266.

Kennewell, S., Tanner, H., Jones, S. and Beauchamp, G. (2008) 'Analysing the use of interactive technology to implement interactive teaching', *Journal of Computer Assisted Learning* 24(1): 61–73.

Kinchin, I. M., de Leij, F. A. A. M. and Hay, D. B. (2005) 'The evolution of a collaborative concept mapping activity for undergraduate microbiology students', *Journal of Further and Higher Education* 29(1): 1–14.

Kinchin, I. M. and Hay, D. B. (2000) 'How a qualitative approach to concept map analysis can be used to aid learning by illustrating patterns of conceptual development', *Educational Research* 42(1): 43–57.

Knobel, M. (2006) 'Technokids, Koala Trouble and Pokemon: literacy, new technologies and popular culture in children's everyday lives', in J. Marsh and E. Millard (eds.) *Popular Literacies: Childhood and Schooling* (pp. 11–28), London: Routledge.

Knox, J. (2007) 'Visual-verbal communication on online newspaper home pages', *Visual Communication* 6(1): 19–53.

Krascum, R., Tregenza, C. and Whitehead, P. (1996) 'Hidden-feature inclusions in children's drawings: the effects of age and model familiarity', *British Journal of Developmental Psychology* 14: 441–455.

Kress, G. (1993) 'Against arbitrariness: the social production of the sign as a foundational issue in critical discourse analysis', *Discourse and Society* 4(2): 169–191.

———. (1995) *Writing the Future: English and the making of a Culture of Innovation*, Sheffield: NATE.

———. (1997) *Before Writing: Rethinking the Paths to Literacy*, London: Routledge.

———. (2000) 'Design and transformation: new theories of meaning', in B. Cope and M. Kalantzis (eds.) *Multiliteracies: Literacy Learning and the Design of Social Futures* (pp. 153–161), London: Routledge.

———. (2003) *Literacy in the New Media Age*, London: Routledge.

———. (2007) 'Thinking about meaning and learning in a world of instability and multiplicity', *Pedagogies* 2(1): 19–34.

———. (2010) *Multimodality: A Social Semiotic Approach to Contemporary Communication*, London: Routledge.

Kress, G., Jewitt, C., Ogborn, J. and Tsatsarelis, C. (2001) *Multimodal Teaching and Learning: The Rhetorics of the Science Classroom*, London: Continuum.

Kress, G. and Van Leeuwen, T. (2001) *Multimodal Discourse: The Modes and Media of Contemporary Communication*, London: Arnold.

———. (2006) *Reading Images: The Grammar of Visual Design* (2nd ed.), London: Routledge.

Lancaster, L. (2001) 'Staring at the page: the functions of gaze in a young child's interpretation of symbolic forms', *Journal of Early Childhood Literacy* 1(2): 131–152.

———. (2007) 'Representing the ways of the world: how children under three start to use syntax in graphic signs', *Journal of Early Childhood Literacy* 7(2): 123–154.

Lankshear, C. and Knobel, M. (2003) *New Literacies: Changing Knowledge and Classroom Learning*, Maidenhead, Berkshire: Open University Press.

Lee, M. (1989) 'When is an object not an object? The effect of 'meaning' upon the copying of line drawings', *British Journal of Psychology* 80: 15–37.

Lemke, J. L. (2000) 'Multimedia literacy demands of the scientific curriculum', *Linguistics and Education* 10(3): 247–271.

———. (1990) *Talking Science: Language, Learning and Values*, Westport, Connecticut: Ablex.

———. (1998) 'Multiplying meaning: visual and verbal semiotics in scientific text', in J. R. Martin and R. Veel (eds.), *Reading Science: Critical and Functional Perspectives on Discourse of Science* (pp. 87–113), London: Routledge.

Lewin, C., Scrimshaw, P., Somekh, B. and Haldane, M. (2009) 'The impact of formal and informal professional development opportunities on primary teachers' adoption of interactive whiteboards', *Technology, Pedagogy and Education* 18(2): 173–185.

Livingstone, S. and Bovill, M. (2001) *Children and their Changing Media Environment: A European Comparative Study*, Mahwah, New Jersey: Lawrence Erlbaum Associates.

Lowenfeld, V. (1939) *The Nature of Creative Activity* (trans. O. A. Oeser), London: Kegan Paul, Trench, Trubner and Co.

Lowenfeld, V. and Brittain, W. L. (1987) *Creative and Mental Growth* (8th ed.), New York: Macmillan Publishing.

Luquet, G. H. (1913) *Les dessins d'un enfant*, Paris: Alcan.

Mahalski, P. A. (1995) 'What happens when students copy notes with different content and layout from an overhead screen? How often do they glance up and how accurate are they?', *British Journal of Educational Technology* 26(1): 5–15.

Marsh, J. (2004) 'Moving stories: digital editing in the nursery', in J. Evans (ed.) *Literacy Moves On: Using Popular Culture, New Technologies and Critical Literacy in the Primary Classroom* (pp. 31–47), London: David Fulton.

Marsh, J. and Millard, E. (2000) *Literacy and Popular Culture: Using Children's Culture in the Classroom*, London: Paul Chapman.

Matthewman, S. and Triggs, P. (2004) ''Obsessive compulsive font disorder': the challenge of supporting pupils' writing with the computer', *Computers and Education* 43(1–2): 125–135.

Matthews, J. (1998) 'The representation of events and objects in the drawings of young children from Singapore and London: implications for the curriculum', *Early Years* 19(1): 90–109.

———. (1999) *The Art of Childhood and Adolescence: The Construction of Meaning*, London: Falmer Press.

Mavers, D. (2009) 'Teaching and learning with a visualiser in the primary classroom: modelling graph-making', *Learning, Media and Technology* 34(1): 11–26.

Mavers, D., Somekh, B. and Restorick, J. (2002) 'Interpreting the externalised images of pupils' conceptions of ICT: methods for the analysis of concept maps', *Computers and Education* 38: 187–207.

Merchant, G. (2003) 'E-mail me your thoughts: digital communication and narrative writing', *Reading* 37(3): 104–110.

———. (2005) 'Digikids: cool dudes and the new writing', *E-Learning* 2(1): 50–60.

Millard, E. (2004) 'Writing about heroes and villains: fusing children's knowledge about popular fantasy texts with school-based literacy requirements', in J. Evans (ed.) *Literacy Moves On: Using Popular Culture, New Technologies and Critical Literacy in the Primary Classroom* (pp. 144–164), London: David Fulton.

Millard, E. and Marsh, J. (2001) 'Words with pictures: the role of visual literacy in writing and its implication for schooling', *Reading* 35(2): 54–61.

Miller, D. and Glover, D. (2002) 'The interactive whiteboard as a force for pedagogic change: the experience of five elementary schools in an English education authority', *Information Technology in Childhood Education Annual 2002* 1: 5–19.

Moss, G. (2001) 'To work or play? Junior age non-fiction as objects of design', *Reading* 35(3): 106–110.

Newfield, D. (2009) *Transmodal Semiosis in Classrooms: Case Studies from South Africa*, PhD Thesis, Institute of Education, University of London, London.

Novak, J. D. and Cañas, A. J. (2006) *The Theory Underlying Concept Maps and How To Construct Them: Technical Report IHMC CMap Tools 2006–01*, Pensacola, Florida: Florida Institute for Human and Machine Cognition.

Novak, J. D. and Gowin, D. B. (1984) *Learning How to Learn*, Cambridge: Cambridge University Press.

O'Toole, M. (1994) *The Language of Displayed Art*, London: Leicester University Press.

Oakeshott, W. (1981) *The Two Winchester Bibles*, Oxford Clarendon Press: Oxford.

Olson, D. R. (1970) *Cognitive Development: The Child's Acquisition of Diagonality*, London: Academic Press.

Ong, W. J. (1982) *Orality and Literacy: The Technologizing of the World*, London: Methuen.

Ormerod, F. and Ivanic, R. (2002) 'Materiality in children's meaning-making practices', *Visual Communication* 1(1): 65–91.

Paget, G. W. (1932) 'Some drawings of men and women made by children of certain non-European races', *Journal of the Royal Anthropological Institute of Great Britain and Ireland* 62: 127–144.

Pahl, K. (1999) *Transformations: Meaning Making in Nursery Education*, Stoke-on-Trent: Trentham Books.

———. (2001) 'Texts as artefacts crossing sites: map making at home and school', *Reading* 35(3): 120–125.

———. (2004) 'Narratives, artifacts and cultural identities: an ethnographic study of communicative practices in the home', *Linguistics and Education* 15: 339–358.

Parkes, M. B. (1991) *Scribes, Scripts and Readers: Studies in the Communication, Presentation and Dissemination of Medieval Texts*, London: The Hambledon Press.

Pearson, M. and Somekh, B. (2003) 'Concept-mapping as a research tool: a study of primary children's representations of information and communication technologies (ICT)', *Education and Information Technologies* 8(1): 5–22.

Phillips, W. A., Hobbs, S. B. and Pratt, F. R. (1978) 'Intellectual realism in children's drawings of cubes', *Cognition* 6: 15–33.

Piaget, J. (1929) *The Child's Conception of the World* (trans. J. Tomlinson and. A. Tomlinson), London: Routledge, Kegan Paul, Trench and Trubner.

Piaget, J. and Inhelder, B. (1956) *The Child's Conception of Space* (trans. F.J. Langdon and J. L. Lunzer), London: Routledge and Kegan Paul.

Porte, G. K. (1995) 'Writing wrongs: copying as a strategy for underachieving EFL writers', *ELT* 49(2): 144–151.

Prout, A. and James, A. (1997) 'A new paradigm for the sociology of childhood? Provenance, promise and problems', in A. James and A. Prout (eds.) *Constructing and Reconstructing Childhood: Contemporary Issues in the Sociological Study of Childhood* (pp. 7–33), London: RoutledgeFalmer.

Rice, D. C., Ryan, J. M. and Samson, S. M. (1998) 'Using concept maps to assess student learning in the science classroom: must different methods compete?', *Journal of Research in Science Teaching* 35(10): 1103–1127.

Royce, T. (2002) 'Multimodality in the TESOL classroom: exploring visual-verbal synergy', *TESOL Quarterly* 36(2): 191–205.

Saussure, F. de (1966) *Course in General Linguistics* (trans. W. Baskin), New York: McGraw-Hill Book Company.

Sedgwick, F. (2002) *Enabling Children's Learning Through Drawing*, London: David Fulton.

Selander, S. (2008) 'Designs for learning: a theoretical perspective', *Designs for Learning* 1(1): 10–22.

Sheppard, E., Ropar, D. and Mitchell, P. (2005) 'The impact of meaning and dimensionality on the accuracy of children's copying', *British Journal of Developmental Psychology* 23: 365–381.

Smith, F. (1984) *Reading Like a Writer*, Reading: The Centre for the Teaching of Reading.

Smith, F., Hardman, F. and Higgins, S. (2006) 'The impact of interactive whiteboards on teacher-pupil interaction in the national literacy and numeracy strategies', *British Educational Research Journal* 32(3): 443–457.

Snyder, I. (2001) 'Hybrid vigour: reconciling the verbal and the visual in electronic communication', in A. Loveless and V. Ellis (eds.) *ICT, Pedagogy and the Curriculum: Subject to Change* (pp. 41–59), London: RoutledgeFalmer.

Somekh, B., Lewin, C., Mavers, D., Fisher, T., Harrison, C., Haw, K., Lunzer, E., McFarlane, A. and Scrimshaw, P. (2002) *ImapCT2: Pupils' and Teachers' Perceptions of ICT in the Home, School and Community*, London: Department for Education and Science.

Somekh, B. and Mavers, D. (2003) 'Mapping learning potential: students' conceptions of ICT in their world', *Assessment in Education* 10(3): 409–420.

Stein, P. (2008) *Multimodal Pedagogies in Diverse Classrooms: Representation, Rights and Resources*, London: Routledge.

Stockl, H. (2005) 'Typography: body and dress of a text—a signing mode between language and image', *Visual Communication* 4(2): 204–214.

Stoddart, T., Abrams, R., Gasper, E. and Canaday, D. (2000) 'Concept maps as assessment in science inquiry learning: a report of methodology', *International Journal of Science Education* 22(12): 1221–1246.

Stow, W. (1997) 'Concept mapping: a tool for self-assessment?', *Primary Science Review* 49: 12–15.

Street, B. V. (1984) *Literacy in Theory and Practice*, Cambridge: Cambridge University Press.

Tekkaya, C. (2003) 'Remediating high school students' misconceptions concerning diffusion and osmosis through concept mapping and conceptual change text', *Research in Science and Technological Education* 21(1): 5–16.

The New London Group (2000) 'A pedagogy of multiliteracies: designing social futures', in B. Cope and M. Kalantzis (eds.) *Multiliteracies: Literacy Learning and the Design of Social Futures* (pp. 9–37), London: Routledge.

Unsworth, L. (2001) *Teaching Multiliteracies across the Curriculum: Changing Contexts of Text and Image in Classroom Practice*, Buckingham: Open University Press.

———. (2006) 'Towards a metalanguage for multiliteracies education: describing the meaning-making resources of language-image interaction', *English Teaching: Practice and Critique* 5(1): 55–76.

Van Leeuwen, T. (2005a) *Introducing Social Semiotics*, Abingdon: Routledge.

———. (2005b) 'Typographic meaning', *Visual Communication* 4(2): 137–143.

Ventola, E. (2006) *Selling Mozart in Salzburg*, paper presented at the Third International Conference on Multimodality (TICOM), University of Pavia, Italy (May, 2006).

Vygotsky, L. S. (1978) *Mind in Society: The Development of Higher Psychological Processes*, Cambridge, Massachusetts: Harvard University Press.

Waller, R. (1996) 'Typography and discourse', in R. Barr, M. L. Kamil, P. Mosenthal and P. D. Pearson (eds.) *Handbook of Reading Research Volume II* (pp. 341–380), Mahwah, New Jersey: Lawrence Erlbaum Associates.

West, T. and Rostvall, A.–L. (2003) 'A study of interaction and learning in instrumental teaching', *International Journal of Music Education* 40(1): 16–27.

Wilson, B. and Ligtvoet, J. (1992) 'Across time and cultures: stylistic changes in the drawings of Dutch children', in D. Thistlewood (ed.) *Research Design and Development* (pp. 75–88), Harlow, Essex: Longman.

Wolf, D. and Perry, M. D. (1988) 'From endpoints to repertoires: some new conclusions about drawing development', *Journal of Aesthetic Education* 22(1): 17–34.

Wray, D. and Lewis, M. (1997) *Extending Literacy: Children Reading and Writing Non-Fiction*, London: Routledge.

Wyatt-Smith, C. and Castleton, G. (2005) 'Examining how teachers judge student writing: an Australian case study', *Journal of Curriculum Studies* 37(2): 131–154.

Zammit, K. and Downes, T. (2002) 'New learning environments and the multiliterate individual: a framework for educators', *Australian Journal of Language and Literacy* 25(2): 24–36.

Index

Page numbers in *italics* denote figures

A

amending what is 'wrong' 48–50
angle 4, 22, 83, 97, 111, 120
Anglo Saxon England 61
animation 13, 49–50, 56, 117–22
apostrophes 54–5
arrows 45, 64, 83; showing magnetic
    force with 67–72, *65–66, 68–9,*
    101
assessment: formative 127; peer 93;
    teachers' 26, 29, 33–4, 36, 42, 47,
    53, 72, 75, 93, 99, 125, 126, 127
assessment criteria 29, 42

B

brevity 52, 92

C

capitalization 17, 23, 53–4, 114
chaining, metaphor of 102
change 5: handling of 126–7
children: discourses on inadequacy 2;
    regarding of as social agents
    2–3, 50
choice 7,8,14,18,30, 36, 44, 46, 48, 49,
    55, 56, 73, 82, 86, 89, 91, 102,
    106
collaborative text making 49–50, *51,*
    117–8
colour/colouring 1, 21, 22, 23, 29, 30,
    36, 44, 45, 55, 56, 60, 70, 84,
    91, 96, 97, 110, 111, 117
combination 5,9,22,36, 46, 56, 73, 80,
    88, 91, 92, 101, 102, 106, 107,
    111, 114, 121
communicational interaction: 'getting it
    wrong' 58–64
'Computers in my world' 75–88, *76,*
    78, 79, 81, 85, 87, 107–8, *108*

concept mapping 75, 79, 82, 84, 86
copying 10, 12–31, 106; denigration
    of in schools 12–13; and digital
    technologies 13; and graphic
    emphasis 23; identically in 12,
    15, 16, 17, 22, 23, 28, 29, 30;
    ideologies of 12–14; 'inaccura-
    cies' in copied writing 19–21;
    intensification and additions 22,
    23–5; and intramodal redesign
    22–23, 28–30; of long multipli-
    cation 15–16, *17*; and meaning
    making 17–18, 20, 22, 23, 24,
    26, 31; and multimodal redesign
    24–25; photocopying and scan-
    ning 15; precision in 19–20; and
    re-production 14–21, 28–9, 31;
    and recontextualisation 25–30;
    and redesign 21–5, 28, 29–30,
    31; social semiotic perspective
    15, 30, 31; substitution within
    and across resource sets 22–23;
    and web page creation 13–14
copywriting 12
corrections 5, 49
criteriality 24, 28, 44, 53, 82, 97, 106;
    shifts in 82–4
curricular subject: framing of the 73,
    102–3
curricular work 13, 90, 93, 118; teach-
    ers' assessment of 34, 42, 75
curriculum 4, 5, 33, 72, 73, 97, 103,
    123, 127, 128; assessment criteria
    42; and drawing 33, 42, 125–6;
    and formal writing 53, 54

D

diagrammatic structuring 75, 80, 88, 89
digital literacy 6

digital technologies 6: challenges to primacy of writing 126; and copying 13; and multimodal text making 5–6

digital writing 52–7; and punctuation 54–5; and spelling 53; typographical options 55–6; use of stickies 52–5, 58

drawing: 'copied' 24–30; and the curriculum 33, 42, 125–6; interactions around 37–40, *41*; lack of formative feedback on 42; making writing into 107–11, *108*, *109*; and motion 34–35; provenance *95*, 96–98, relationship with writing 99; talking about by children 38; reteachers' response and assessment of in classroom 33–4, 36–37; and semiotic work 32

dry-wipe whiteboards 92, 93–4, *93*, 98, 102

durability of texts 90

E

economy, representational/semiotic 52, 74, 83, 89, 94, 107, 111

educational policy 33

egocentrism 58

email 58–64, *59*, *62*; and power relations 63–4; and spacing 61–3, *62*; and spelling 59–60

embodied knowledge 60

embodied representation/texts 6, 48, 50, 99, 100, 105

erasing 15, 49, 70, 71, 84, 92

errors *see* 'getting it wrong'

European *Représentation* project 72, 82

exclamation marks 55, 115

F

feedback 34, 39, 42, 64, 73, 125

fire, drawing of 110–111

fireworks 36, *37*

fleeting texts 90–104

framing/frames and assessment 29, 42; and copying 25; of classroom practices 93–4; of the curricular subject 30, 73, 102–3; graphic 23, 28; ideological 3, 12, 30, 64, 124; of medium 44–45; 90–2; of mode 98–102; pedagogic 94–6, *95*; and punctuation 22; of purpose and social relations 7, 8, 9, 31, 50,55, 124; and recognition 3, 22, 129; responding to prior 96–8; separation as means of 61, 62, 75; of task 25, 76, 128

full stops 28, 53–4, 62, 114

G

genres 5, 54, 58, 61, 74, 75, 102, 105

'getting it wrong' 48–73; and amending 48–50; in communicational interaction 58–64; as 'getting it right' 50–8; and online sticky writing 52–8; showing magnetic force with arrows 64–73, *68–9*

Gowin, D.B. 84

graphic emphasis: and copying 23; and meaning 89

H

heart message 45–6, *46*

Holy Sprit: drawing of 110–11

human body: drawing of 4, 38; changing postures of 34–5

hypertextual links 14, 128

I

ideology: and recognition 124–6

ImpaCT2 evaluation 75, 84, 112

inaccuracies: and copied writing 19–21

Inhelder, Bärbel 20

interaction: 'getting it wrong' in communicational 58–64

interpretation 3, 5, 9, 10, 12, 32, 37–8, 47, 53, 57, 58, 59, 60, 64, 67, 73, 75, 80, 86, 89, 94, 96, 97, 98, 104, 106, 107, 111, 112, 116, 123, 124; and copying 12, 15, 16, 17, 18, 21, 22, 23, 29; demanding of semiotic work 47

J

Japan: copying in 12

jumble 74–81, 88

K

Kress, Gunther 4, 9

L

labelling 14, 70, 75, 83, 86–89, 97, 103

language 57

layout 14, 74, 76, 79, 84, 89, 97; copying of 22, 28; and meaning making 89; and transcription 115–16

learning, signs of 99
lens, directing the 10–11; ideology of the 2–3; for investigating 6–9; on the unremarkable 3–6
letter case 53–4
line endpoints 36
lines 4, 22, 32, 34, 36, 98, 101, in copying 20, 29; of writing 28, 56
linguistic cohesion 99
links in mapping, linkage 75–80, 86–7, 89
literacy 4–6, 33, 53, 57–58, 117, 119, 125; and copying 28–30
long multiplication: copying of 16, *17*
Luquet, Georges-Henri 20

M

magnets: dry-wipe whiteboard text 92, 94, *95*, 96, 97–101, 103; using arrows to show force of *65*, 66–72, *68–9*
mapping 72, 74–89, *81*, *85*, *87*, 107–8, *108*; concept 75, 79, 82, 84, 86; mind 75, 79, 86, 96
marking: by teachers 34, 42
materiality 15, 22, 44–5, 56, 84, 90, 91, 110, 114
meaning: modal distribution of 100–1, *101*; in the unnoticed 32–7
meaning making 10, 37–42, 47, 92, 124; and act of production 18; and copying 17–18, 20, 22, 23, 24, 26, 31; as fluid and dynamic 102; teachers' engagement with children's 127; with what has been discarded 44–6
medieval England 53, 91
medium: choice of 91; framing of 90–2; making meaning with 44–45; shaping of text making by specification of 92; use of as socially regulated 91–2
messiness 11, 59, 74, 75, 88, 124
metalanguage 128
metaphor 45, 55, 63, 86, 102, 103, 107–10, 115, 122
mind mapping 75, 79, 86, 96
'mistakes' 1, 4, 11, 16, 21, 22, 60–1, 63, 64, 71, 107, 114, 117, 125 *see also* 'getting it wrong'
modal loading 75
mode: framing of 98–102; representation of 6, 7, 9, 22, 42, 64, 88, 104, 116, 119, 127; shifts across 104, 105, 106, 111, 112, 116, 123
movement: in animation 50, 119–121; representing of in drawing 34–6 39, 40, 110; and in arrows 64, 66, 67, 101
multimodality 6, 49–50, 89, 96–7, 99, 101–2, 104, 118, 123
'Mum is my Hirow' 1, 2, 5, 8

N

Novak, J.D. 84

O

online environment 14: and messaging 58–64, *59*; and sticky writing 50–5, 58; *see also* web pages
ordinariness 1, 8, 9, 10, 32–47, 53, 54, 91, 96, 104, 111, 123, 124
orientation 1, 29, 50, 64, 86–7, 96, 99, 100
osmosis 40, 42, *43*

P

paper 1, 15, 16, 44, 45, 90, 91
pedagogic framing 94–6, *95*
pencil pressure 36
pencils 45, 91, 92, 106, 110
pens 45, 92, 93
Pentecost 108–11, *109*
photocopying 15
Piaget, Jean 20
power relations: and email exchange 63–4
presentation 74, 84, 89; semiotics of 55
principled 4, 5, 7, 9, 23, 28, 30, 44, 48, 59, 60, 61, 62, 63, 70, 73, 75, 79, 85, 115, 123, 127
primary education 96
prior framing 118; responding to 96–8
provenance 30, 104; semiotic 7, 8, 39
punctuation 53–4; and sticky writing 54–5; and transcription 114–15

Q

question marks 55, 114

R

'reading pathways' 79–80
recognition 14, 46, 112; and ideology 124–6
recontextualization: and copying 25–30
redesign 123, 124; and copying 16, 21–6, 28, 29–30, 31; intramodal

22, 23, 30; of narrative as action-only animation 117–20, 122; and transcription 112, 115; transmodal 97, 106, 111, 122, 123

remaking 105–23; making a stop-frame animation from storyboards 117–22, *118*; making writing into drawing 107–12, *108*, *109*; representation 105–6; and textus of semiotic resources 123; and transcription 112–17

remarkable: lens on in children's drawing and writing 3–6

remediation 15, 106

repetition 34, 50, 74, 103, 114, 117; and concept maps 84–8, *85*

representation 3–7, 31, 32, 73, 81, 91, 94, 124; and assessment criteria in curriculum 42; drawing as a mode of seen as inadequate 125–8; and embodiment 39–40, 99; and materiality 44–5, 110–11; remaking 105–6; social semiotic perspective 15, 22, 32, 37, 60

re-production 103; and copying 14–21, 24, 26, 28–9, 31

resemioticization 106, 123

resourcefulness 5

S

Saussure, Ferdinand de 6, 7

scale 15, 75, 78, 89, 92, 94, 96

scanning 15

science curriculum 96, 102–3; and copying 25, 30; and drawing 36

'scribble' 3, 4, 111

seasons 33–4, *35*

semiosis 92, 102, 124

semiotic chain 92, 102

semiotic load 7, 50, 126

semiotic pathways 104

semiotic plenitude 10, 37, 39, 47, 61, 63, 88, 91, 116

semiotic reservoirs 89, 127

semiotic resources 4, 6, 7–9, 22, 38–9, 46, 54, 57, 58, 63, 73, 81, 89, 106, 115, 123, 127; arrows as 64; silence as 63

semiotic settling 9, 49, 83, 92, 102, 124

semiotic work 9, 10, 12, 15, 30, 32, 34, 36, 47, 73, 74, 90, 92, 96, 104, 105, 106, 107, 111, 119, 123, 124, 129

semiotics 6, 7–8, 106

semiotics setting 9, 49, 83, 92, 102, 124

sensations: depicting of 4

shading 4, 30, 36, 40, 45, 70, 78, 97, 110

shorthand 53, 74, 75, 76, 82–4, 88

signifying resources 8, 21, 23, 44, 89, 106

signs 6, 7, 15, 22, 37, 49, 88. *See also* social semiotic perspective

sign complex 56, 57, 84, 88, 111

silence: as semiotic resource 63

social semiotic perspective 6, 7, 38, 48, 58; and copying 15, 31, 32; and representation 15, 22, 32, 37, 39, 44–5

space/spacing: between words in email 61–2, *62*, 63; and copying 23, 29; and the graphic surface 10, 52, 55, 70, 92, 115; and mapping 74, 75, 78, 79, 83, 85

spelling 4–5, 53, 59–62, 112; and sticky writing 53

sticky writing: and online environment 52–6, 58

stop-frame animation 117–22

storyboard: making a stop-frame animation from a 117–22, *118*

strokes, of pencil 36, 110, 111

subject matter: 9–10, 13, 16, 25, 31, 57, 62, 97, 111

substances 15, 30, 44–45, 90, 91–2, 110–11

surfaces 15, 44–6, 90, 91–2

T

teachers: assessment by 24, 33–4, 37, 42, 75, 93, 99, 125, 127; engagement with children's meaning making 40, 94; instruction/demonstration 33, 63, *65*, 67, 96, 97 marking by 34, 42, 60

text: term of 8

text making 8–9; co-presence of writing and drawing 6, 9; collaborative 49–50, *51*; definition 8; digital technology and multimodal 5–6; in oral silence 17, 21; as principled 9, 48, 61, 73; richness of children's 46, 83; as social action 9, 31, 50, 73

texting 53, 54, 55, 56, 57

three-dimensionality 32

transcript, making a 112–17, *113*

transcription 21, 49, 60, 63
transduction 106, 107
transmodalism 106; transmodal rede-
    sign 111, 122, 124
typographical resources: and digital
    writing 55–6

U
unnoticed, meaning in the 32–7
unremarkable, lens on 3–6

V
visualiser 17, 67, 71–2, *95*, 96
Vygotsky, L.S. 44

W
Wallace and Gromit 117

web: copying and pasting from 23
web pages 6, 74, 126; creation of
    13–14, 52
white space 28, 61, 70, 78, 79, 115
whiteboards *see* dry-wipe whiteboards
whole-class teaching 27, 67, 93, 94,
    96
wind, drawing of 34, 110
writing: assessment of 42, 72; challeng-
    ing of by digital technologies
    126; copying 18–20, 23, 28–29;
    curriculum and formal 52–4, 58,
    61–2; as design 56–7; digital 55;
    making into drawing 107–12,
    108, *109*; resources of 22;
    sequentiality in 38
written narratives 119

LRC
NEW COLLEGE
WITHDRAWN

T - #0081 - 160719 - C0 - 229/152/9 - PB - 9780415846448